Hanns Eisler
A Rebel in Music

INTERNATIONAL PUBLISHERS
381 Park Avenue South NEW YORK, N.Y. 10016

Hanns Eisler
A Rebel in Music

Editor
Manfred Grabs

Hanns Eisler
A Rebel in Music

Selected Writings

Edited and
with an Introduction by
Manfred Grabs

International Publishers
New York

Published simultaneously by
International Publishers, New York
and Seven Seas Books, Berlin, 1978

Marjorie Meyer
Translator

Library of Congress Cataloging in Publication Data
Eisler, Hanns, 1898–1962.
A rebel in music.
1. Music–Addresses, essays, lectures.
I. Title.
ML60.E4   780'.8   76-55331
ISBN 0-7178-0486-0

Contents

Introduction
Music for the New World
in the Forming

When the great names of music of our time are counted the name of Hanns Eisler must be included among them. We talk of the "classical" composers of modern music and think first of Schönberg, Stravinsky, Bartók and Shostakovich. Each of these names stands for a particular style and original feature in the growth of modern music.

At present, opinion on Hanns Eisler is still divided. However, today it can hardly be denied that his oeuvre is an artistic achievement of historic significance.

Eisler was an artist in a transitional period. He came from a liberal-bourgeois background, but nonetheless took up the ideas and aims of the revolutionary working-class movement. He worked in a bourgeois society, but opposed its system, ideology and also the trends of its art. He was faced with the difficult and contradictory task of creating music that could be absorbed by the working class, used in the struggle against exploitation and the danger of fascism and yet without sacrificing aesthetic standards. Only in the last years of his life in the German Democratic Republic did he have the satisfaction of modifying his fighting point of view and feeling at one with the society in which he worked.

Dmitri Shostakovich said of Eisler, "He will remain for all of us the magnificent example of a musician who was always to be found in the front ranks and who actively used his creative powers for progress and peace, in the struggle for a new and just society and for a better future. Together with the flaming words of the revolutionary tribunes, his music forced its way into life. His songs were the favorite, well tried weapon of the proletariat."

An artist like Eisler could scarcely count on recognition from the bourgeois art apologists, indeed it was more likely that he could count on slander or ignorance. But, in the opinion of Hans Heinz Stuckenschmidt, anyone who had not become completely blinded by anti-Communism could see that by 1930 Eisler was playing "a singular role" in music life and that "without figuring in the programs of bourgeois concerts," he was one of the "most frequently performed composers and moreover a popular figure among the working people." This same musicologist, however, later became a protagonist of those who claimed that Eisler as a representative of socialist music culture in the G.D.R. was opposed to "purely political and ideological Party aesthetics." Hoping to find a dissident in disguise, the first publication of Eisler's works outside the socialist countries appeared in 1970 in the Federal Republic of Germany. After the breakdown of the boycott of Brecht, Eisler was also taken up there by the theater and discussion circles, as his music was such an integral part of Brecht's works. Alongside the growing class differences in imperialist countries resulting from the recent crisis of capitalism, there was a revival of the works of the first great master of revolutionary proletarian music. Due to the sudden widespread interest, Eisler's works became respectable for bourgeois musicology. They recalled the praise that Schönberg had heaped on Eisler, naming him together with Berg and Webern as "the most talented young composers with the best training whom I have taught." Thus Eisler became a notable figure of the New Vienna School. To some, his dilemma had only been that in addition to his worthwhile compositions, influenced by Schönberg, he had to busy himself as a Communist agitator.

When Eisler discovered that politics concerned itself with music it was logical that he, as a musician, concerned himself with politics. He recognized that a system of society which degrades music to a commodity and isolates it from the masses is reprehensible and must be opposed, since it harms man and art. That is why Eisler allied himself with the leading force of the working class, whose historic task it is to change relations from top to bottom and to create a new and nobler order. He did not consider this decision a special virtue on his part. "We had no other chance. We can only go over to the bourgeoisie or to our working class which has brought us up ... Pupils follow the master," Eisler acknowledged. He did not consider himself only a pupil, but equally a messenger of the working class, "who arrives out of breath, with something to hand over." "The idea of handing something over, of being a messenger who runs, and who has a message to deliver, has, since my youth, actually been the greatest idea that I learned from the working class ... To do something useful, that can be handed over."

He was not satisfied just to observe but mixed with the demonstrators and sang his own songs with them. He accompanied agit-prop groups into the backyards and meeting rooms, he attended the meetings of the workers, performing together with Ernst Busch, "the Richard Tauber of the barricades," and he worked closely with the workers' choir movement. When his big oratorio-style didactic play, *Die Massnahme* (The Measures Taken–text by Brecht) was first performed in December 1930 at the Berlin Philharmonic Hall, he was to be found singing in the choir.

Eisler's songs surmounted all boundaries. In the Soviet Union they were a stimulant to the workers in their great tasks. Workers in London, Paris and Detroit sang them as well as soldiers of the Eighth Route Army in China. During the Spanish Civil War Eisler's songs radiated courage and confidence. It is not without significance that this uncompromising musician, experienced in the struggle, wrote the national anthem for the first socialist state on German soil. Eisler's proletarian fighting songs, voicing the demands of the working class from a Marxist-Leninist point of view like the *Solidaritätslied* and the *Einheitsfrontlied*, stand next to hymns of freedom and human justice such as the

Marseillaise, the *Internationale* and *Workers, Unite for the Battle!*

For Eisler music and art in general were "a tutor in the class struggle." His ideas on the function of music nonetheless did not imply any restriction in the use of the various genres, or in the quality of the material and thematic multiplicity—certainly not for a musician of Eisler's eminence. On the contrary, the diverse demands made of a musician closely linked to reality acted as a spur to express himself in a multitude of ways. Thus, his vocal works range from unaccompanied children's songs to orchestral song cycles, from elementary marching songs to the sophisticated structure of concert songs, from a quickly written chanson to the demanding bigger forms of cantata and oratorio. Many songs are integral parts of film music, especially of incidental music, and a number of Brecht's plays are unimaginable without Eisler's music. Eisler's symphonic and chamber music, like his vocal works for concerts, were not written for the bourgeois concert business. Even this music is politically "suspicious," because of its often provocative character and its stirring and disquieting manner of expression. Small wonder, then, that even today it is so difficult for these works to find acceptance in bourgeois circles.

Like few other composers Eisler was a remarkable theoretician as well as a skillful author. He wrote a number of poems and a libretto to a Faust opera, unfortunately not composed. It was his habit to take texts by other poets, from Hölderlin to Brecht and to adapt them effectively and cleverly for his compositions.

As a theoretician on aesthetic questions he had in view not so much his own creative works as independent aesthetic ideas on the social function of music. These he then put into effect. Moreover, Eisler's cultural-political and aesthetic ideas were of especial value because they were the product of an experienced and critical musician. Thus, his aesthetics are not abstract; even when dealing with new trends and qualities in music they are always a reflection of real possibilities. They are part of a dialectical, varied and personal engagement in building a socialist music culture. Eisler's contributions to a Marxist music aesthetics were not written with a view to establishing a complete conception of music aesthetics. They were written as reactions to actual requirements under different social and historical circumstances and, of course, are influenced by these. This consequently does not exclude contradictions, underlining all the more the dialectics of Eisler's thinking. His ideas may be stimulating and helpful in critically surveying what has been attained, or in solving similar problems today, yet it would be wrong to see them out of their historical context and to apply them mechanically. Rather they should be considered in the light of conditions today and should be further developed.

Eisler wrote for his composer colleagues, for practising musicians and for the general public whom he wished to win over as audience and ally. He did not only talk about music, but also about those for whom it was intended and whom it should serve, about their work, their way of life and their political opinions. He wanted really to bring home the actual problems to his readers or listeners, through the manner of presentation, in order to convince them all the more.

Eisler lectured on "The Crisis in Music" on December 7, 1935, in Town Hall, New York, following which Marc Blitzstein wrote in *New Masses* of June 23, 1936 about Eisler's ideological and aesthetic opinion, saying "Eisler is first a composer; it is good to remember that his formulation, his theories grow out of, have roots in, music. They are your true 'aesthetic,' articulated out of the thing, possessed and actual, not cooked-up, not arbitrary, not nursed along to induce the thing, and make it happen. Schönberg once said of the typical theorizer, 'Nobody watches more closely over his property than the man who knows that, strictly speaking, it does not belong to him.' Eisler's property is his own; he shares it with the working class of the world."

Driven from Germany by fascism, Eisler spent the greater part of his emigration in the United States. His ten American years were an important period of his life and work. It was here that he got to know capitalism in its "most naked, most savage and most brutal form." America seemed to him to be the country "where a dictatorship could be practised without a superstructure, and where generations go to wrack and ruin." "Unless you have seen America," Eisler wrote, "you only know capitalism in part." At the same time he admired the courageous struggle of the progressive forces, and the dynamic nature of life imprinted on the country by the working people. In time his memories of America became more idealistic and were expressed by Faust in his opera libretto: "Past days recalling, I can scarcely say they were pleasant. And yet, Atlanta, how radiant the light of your sun!"

This was also one of his most productive and creative periods. Eisler had a very simple explanation for this—boredom. "Brecht and I also did creative work to avoid becoming bored ... In emigration our greatest inspiration came not only from our understanding of class relationships, our genuine and I hope honorable struggle against fascism and for socialism—but also from boredom—as a Marxist one must be realistic—the tormenting boredom of an exile, who only has himself to think about all day long."

Eisler earned his livelihood mainly as a film composer and teacher. A generous research grant from the Rockefeller Foundation gave him the opportunity to experiment with new potentialities of using music in films.

But at the same time he was working on the large-scale *Deutsche Symphonie* for solos, choir and orchestra. He dedicated his Woodbury Songbook to a school in Woodbury: this is a collection of a-cappella pieces. He wrote piano pieces and composed his Hollywood Songbook, a sort of music diary. Under the emigration restrictions it was no longer possible for him to write works which could be used in the day-to-day political struggle. He worked now for the future, something he had never done before, and for him that meant the time when the working class would have taken power. He himself pointed out later that because of its content and scope, a work like the *Deutsche Symphonie* could only be performed "under the dictatorship of the proletariat, in the form which today we call the German Democratic Republic." This productivity anticipating future social developments in thematic and artistic form documents Eisler's honest and conscious attitude during the difficult years of exile.

Among like-minded people Eisler was respected and highly honored. On the occasion of his first visit to the United States when he gave a lecture and concert tour in aid of anti-fascist solidarity, Joe Foster wrote in the *Daily Worker* of March 1, 1935: "In every city of the world, hundreds of thousands of workers pound along the pavements, voicing in mass protest the outrages and exploitations of their ruling classes. They remember their tortured and imprisoned comrades, the untold sufferings and brutality that has been their lot. As they march, thousands of voices eagerly catch up in militant determined songs their struggles and their fight for liberation. In the pulsating, stirring rhythms of these revolutionary songs they forge their common challenge, which hurls itself in a volume of sound against the very walls of their ruling-class enemies. Behind this music stands Hanns Eisler–foremost revolutionary composer. He is beloved of all the masses of every country. In Prague, Holland, Vienna, Saarbrucken, Paris, London, and in other cities, the masses flock by the thousands to hear him. And no wonder. For his music reflects with complete understanding the reality of their lives, infuses them with courage, and provides a stimulus for further struggle... Naturally he was the first to go, when Hitler came into power. His music was destroyed, his records broken."

The tug of war instituted by the authorities over Eisler's

immigrant visa grew to a disgraceful scandal. For two years Eisler had to fight for this visa. For two years he lived in the uncertainty of not knowing whether he would obtain an extension to his restricted visitor's visa. He was threatened with deportation. When on another occasion his visa had become invalid, a warrant for his arrest was made out and he had to seek safety in Mexico. Eisler finally received his immigrant visa in October 1940, through the support of prominent personalities, including Mrs. Eleanor Roosevelt, the President's wife.

Just as scandalous was the way in which the American administration got rid of their unwanted guest. In the growing anti-Communism and anti-Sovietism after the death of President Roosevelt innumerable progressive artists, including Hollywood film people, were called before the House Committee on Un-American Activities, mostly on the flimsiest of accusations. Hanns Eisler was among them; there was the added complication that his brother, Gerhart, was accused of being a "Moscow agent" and a "Communist spy." Although he, Hanns Eisler, wished to leave the country, he was threatened with being put into a detention camp. A longwinded and undignified hearing, which foresaw deportation if found guilty, was formally terminated under the pressure of a world-wide solidarity campaign, led by the American Committee for Justice for Hanns Eisler.

His friends organized a brilliant farewell concert of his works in his honor. The *Daily News* expressed the wish that Eisler might judge his second home by the behavior of the people who had befriended him and who had stood up for him, but "not by those who would spread hate and intolerance in the name of 'Americanism.'" Eisler always acted in accordance with this wish.

He returned to Berlin, to the part of Germany where he could realize the ideas for which he had fought so long. He helped to build up a socialist music culture with his wealth of experience, with new works and by teaching a great number of composers. There was no lack of high honors, yet for him the highest honor and satisfaction was when his music was performed and understood. For the first time in his life his works became accessible through extensive publication. His trusted friend of many years, Bertolt Brecht, wrote in the preface of the first volume of Eisler's Collected Songs, the order of which he himself arranged: "The basic attitude is revolutionary in the highest sense. This music develops in listeners and players the mighty impulses and understanding of an era where productivity of every kind is the source of all pleasure and morality. It engenders new tenderness and strength, endurance and flexibility, impatience and forethought, a profusion of claims and self-sacrifice . . .

"By taking part in his work you give yourselves up to the motives and prospects of a new world in the forming."

Berlin, 1976   Manfred Grabs

Editor's Note

For this collection we have chosen in the main popularly written articles on the role of music in the process of revolutionary struggles; descriptions of Eisler's experiences with regard to the growth and influence of music in the class struggle as well as articles in connection with his stay in the United States. Specific and detailed analyses have not been included.

The quoted material which Eisler uses is not always quoted literally.

Titles which are not identical with those given in the Sources have been taken from *Hanns Eisler, Gesammelte Werke* (EGW), Volume III–or have been supplemented by the editor.

We have indicated where the original texts may be found in the Collected Works, and have used the abbreviation EGW for Eisler's Collected Works.

For sake of convenience explanatory notes are at the end of each article.

On Old and New Music
1925

What isn't new music accused of! (By new music I mean
music after Richard Strauss.) They say it has no tradition,
is all bluff or is construed; it does away—so they say—with
the musical idea, melody and especially with form. All these
accusations, were they true, would show the differences
between old and new music. But one thing is forgotten,
namely, that the same accusations were leveled against old
music when it was new. Today Mozart is counted among
the easily understandable composers, yet in his time he was
considered complicated, florid and recklessly discordant.
And what about Beethoven's Symphony No. 9, or even
more, his last quartets? It has always been the same when
together with new sound effects a new style appears.

The fact that we wear different clothes today than we
wore five hundred years ago is not questioned, for people
adapt themselves to new ways of living. For a worker
standing at a machine eight hours a day wearing clothes of
the Renaissance would be absurd; as well as an office
worker sitting at his desk in a toga; or a woman wearing a
crinoline. How would she climb into a streetcar got up like
that for example, or get through the bustling crowds throng-
ing the streets today?

None of Schubert's contemporaries made fun of the subject of his song *Die Post*[1] (Mailcoach). Yet people make
fun of the piece *Pacific 231*[2] by Honegger (a young
Swiss-born French composer) before they have heard it,
because it is about an express train. (Here it is not a question of comparing the composers or the compositions but
the subject of the compositions.) Schubert wrote his song

about the mailcoach, not as a "vehicle," but as a "messenger of love." Today mailcoaches no longer exist. You will agree that with the best will in the world the modern musician cannot regard an "express train" as a "messenger of love," although it may well be so, just as Schubert's mailcoach was. But he is fascinated perhaps by the speed of it, the power, or perhaps something else typical of the time. Why, one might ask, shouldn't an express train mean something to a child of his time?

Take another example: the mill was a popular lyrical subject. Countless poems were composed about the mill, the millstream, the miller and the miller's daughter, drawing various conclusions. For the composer today it is more difficult. There are few romantic mills left and who wants to lie down by a stream under a signboard. Today's mill is usually a factory filled with the noise of rushing, pounding and hissing. The composer of earlier days saw his mill as an ornament to nature. Together with the mill he loved its inhabitants and their patriarchal way of life. Today's artist, if he is emotionally honest and thinks clearly, would have to draw quite different conclusions were he confronted with a Mill Company Limited. Possibly he would see hundreds of people working, he would see poverty and distress. Even declarations of love sound different in a factory yard than in nature. And he will be wary of asking today's millstream—the factory waste—whither it is flowing so fast, as Schubert asks his millstream.

The modern artist is impressed by quite different things, accordingly he must feel quite differently. If these different sensations are given a form of expression, then the way of expressing them, the musical configuration will also be different. And the material with which the artist fashions his new ideas will consequently have to change with his changed intentions. This process and the results of it are called "new" by some people and "modern" by others. In reality it is neither new nor modern, only different. Now it would be wrong to believe that the modern artist regards his musical predecessors without respect or with contempt. No one admires the masters of old music more and needs to understand them better than does the modern artist. But this admiration and understanding must never become philistine, rejecting all that differs from the old school.

No one needs to understand them better?

No branch of art in the world has ever broken completely with the work of its predecessors. Elements common to the past can always be found even in works decried as "radical." Not only are the older forms frequently used (concerto grosso, fugue, suite; in opera the aria and recitative), but also in details the continuity from classical or pre-classical music can be seen. You may judge from this that today's artist must have had a very comprehensive schooling with a profound comprehension of the work of his predecessors. To be able to play an instrument and have a superficial knowledge of music of the past, are not enough. He himself must have experienced the whole development of music in order to move freely in his art. No matter how much the presentation of an art may change, the criteria for the work of art itself will always remain the same. Whether about a mill or a Mill Company Limited is immaterial when all is said and done. In the end the listener will only ask himself, did the composer have a musical idea and was he able to give shape to it? The question of a triad in C major or a new chord is equally immaterial. The main thing will always be—whether the artist can express with the highest degree of perfection what he wishes to express emotionally.

A further favorite objection to modern music is that it is complicated. How often does one hear, "Modern music is so difficult to understand."

Why is this? Most listeners believe right from the beginning that a quartet by Beethoven is easier to take in and understand than a piece by Stravinsky, for example. It is because the listener always finds some points, even in complicated works by the classical composers, with which a centuries-long musical tradition has made him familiar. It is precisely the lack of this familiarity that makes it hard for the listener to understand modern music, be it ever so primitive! Apart from this he demands from each work a certain type of sound that he is accustomed to (he calls it harmonious), the lack of which estranges him so much. This obstinate adherence to tradition is nowhere to be found so strongly as in art. Thus the real point of division between old and new music is often not the composer, but the listener, for he always wants to hear the same, he always expects the usual emotional effect. If we were to go by the taste of such listeners, then only those works would be played that have already been played a thousand times before, only the thousand and first time probably presented in an inferior interpretation. Indeed, it is not so much a matter of the purely musical effect but the subject of the music. Regrettably the average listener cannot free himself of his "mill." Though "mills" no longer exist he still wants to hear about them again and again. So if an artist like Schönberg comes along and composes *Pierrot* the listener holds up his hands in horror and exclaims, "How can anyone compose a thing like that?" And so from the first he is prejudiced against such a work. This happened to Strauss at the start with his operas *Salome* and *Electra,* and unfortunately it will invariably happen to anyone with enough genius to say something of his own and something new.

Let me say this to all music lovers and music listeners: don't come to a concert only as guardians of cherished traditions. Don't cling to a standard of beauty by which you assess a work, for it may not be what you really feel. Don't look up reference books to see "whether it is right" or whether this chord was "allowed" a hundred years ago. And if you hear a complicated sound, then try to understand it, don't scold the creator. You must not believe that all modern composers are revolutionaries or are poking fun. They simply want to make music, that is all, as our great masters wanted to, young or old. Everyone in his own time and within the framework of that time. That is the whole secret!

Source: *Von alter und neuer Musik* in *Musik und Gegenwart,* a series of leaflets, published by *Musikblätter des Anbruch,* Vienna, No. 3, c. 1925.
EGW III/1, pp. 18–21
This is the oldest existing published article by Eisler.

1   *Die Post,* 13th song in Schubert's song cycle *Die Winterreise.*

2   Arthur Honegger (1892–1955), *Pacific 231,* composed 1923, refers to type of locomotive.

Satirical Aphorisms
1928

Don't think that it is all right nowadays if it is only music of which a musician is ignorant. No, he should aspire to be a passionate ignoramus in every other sphere as well.

Harmony is a myth out of the dawn of history.

Melody is what one always misses.

In their youth musicians are wont to play chamber music. One school of doctors says that it is extraordinarily harmful; the Ministry of Culture should take energetic steps to counter it by educational films such as, "The effects of the solo violin sonata and how to prevent them," and also by distributing hygienic remedies to the Conservatoire students. We cannot call attention sharply enough to the exaggeration of this danger, which only leads to severe nervous breakdowns among young people and can ruin them for life. There is no doubt that up to a certain age, the practice of chamber music can be quite harmless, provided it does not become a habit.

Anyone not capable of composing and who has given up playing an instrument because he is hopeless at it, can become a conductor. What does he need for this profession? Ethos, a baton, a clumsy hand and a wealthy wife. It does not require much technique to disguise one's own inability through threatening looks at the orchestra. Now we have an excessive number of personalities (no talent, no character either), and you only have to spit and straightaway a genius feels hurt. Then quickly a few interesting first performances and the critics immediately write, "Never before have we heard the 'Eroica' like this. That was real Beethoven lashing about with his minor fourth-sixth chords. The diabolical assurance, the suggestive power with which the Master let our gifted horn player Navradil play the difficult passage in the recapitulation was simply overwhelming. This mixture of St. Francis of Assisi and a ghetto Jew conquered the audience with an irresistible force. Unfortunately, we were unable to stay until the end of the interminable applause, because our review had to be in the hands of the editor before midnight."

We sympathize with the conductor's vocation which is like that of a traveling salesman whose social status is unjustly frowned upon. Honestly, it is all the same if by diabolical suggestive power you fool a customer into buying a quantity of cotton goods, or whether you fool the public with Beethoven's symphonies. It is to be deplored that something as important as trade be deprived of these valuable individuals. However, we hope that by applying the principle of mechanical interpretation those concerned will soon be in a position to sell cotton goods.

Polyphony is best explained as follows: four people all start shouting at the same time in order to convince the listener that they have absolutely nothing to say.

Homophony is best explained in the following way: you address a lady, a complete stranger, in the street, walk for hours by her side without saying anything except "Nice weather today" or "You look charming" and after such futile efforts go off in the opposite direction.

Tonality is a means of art still used successfully today in elementary piano teaching.

Source: *Zeitgemässe Betrachtungen*, typescript, Hanns Eisler Archives.

Published in part in *Der Auftakt*, Prague, 1928, Nos. 5 and 6 entitled, *Zeitgemässe Betrachtungen zweier Musiker*.

Selection in *Musik und Gesellschaft*, Berlin, 1958, No. 6, as *Satirische Aphorismen*.

EGW III/1, pp. 82–86.

Of the total of 18 aphorisms 8 are included in this edition. Hans Heinz Stuckenschmidt, given as the co-author of the aphorisms, was at that time a close friend of Eisler's, and later wrote a biography of the composer. Both worked together in the left-wing artists' *Novembergruppe*. A concluding remark to the collection of aphorisms states they were written in March 1927, "in the course of conversations while working together."

On the Situation in Modern Music
1928

For the dutiful gathered round the deathbed, death-rattles are so wearisome they fall asleep. Their snoring sounds similar and so it is difficult to ascertain who is actually dying. That is the relation between bourgeois society and modern music.

You see, music is a strange art. The muse has a physical failing. Her two legs are missing and so she cannot stand or walk on earth and is forced to move in "higher regions" by means of a pair of very defective wings. But now planes and factory smoke are causing a disturbance up there too, and radio listeners curse the atmospherics and the annoying radio hams. However, the somewhat incapacitated muse flutters on bravely, still helping many people to produce an amount of highly questionable goods, questionable because they are of little concern to anybody, not even to those who produce them, questionable because they are mostly not worth the question.

But meanwhile, her much less esteemed sister, entertainment music (that is music to talk to in contrast to serious music), has made herself most conspicuous. She conquers everyone, is at home everywhere, has a more realistic purpose, dancing and Eros, and is well on the way to driving her sister off to heaven.

What the devil! Whoever is off to heaven must have died! That sounds like a lyric, but it is only the cry of distress today of the musician who cannot be deluded about the fact that his art is frightfully isolated and who gets no satisfaction from giving birth to one work after another, merely for the sake of writing. He aspires to something vital, vital because it concerns everyone, and consequently is a vital part of everyone, and he is fed up with helping a few gourmets to procure increasingly esoteric pleasures.

All styles of the past few years whether conscious or subconscious are a result of this knowledge. For example, the new classicism (as though the imitation of a past musical style could restore the social structure from which it sprang), the mechanization of music (as though musical works in society today acquire greater validity if they are conceived or performed on musical automatons), the renaissance in religious music (which would require a renaissance in piety as a preliminary condition) and so on.

The departure from the Romantics can also be traced back to these facts. It was felt that the emotions of one individual were no longer adequate to express something of general validity and so what was wanted was pure music-making, without feeling, without expression, simply a play on tones.

In the end a simple recipe was found. You take elements of entertainment music, mix it with some "serious" music, add a bit of the new classicism, then carefully pour a measure of religiosity over the whole. The result is that we hear the same jazz as in a night-club, only more stylized and not so well done.

Yet all these fashions show how isolation has led to confusion and to rootlessness–a sign of how far the crisis in society is already affecting music.

In addition there are a number of typical features of degeneration. At no time was the craftsman's ability and knowledge at such a low level; at no time were plain incapability and the wildest dilettantism able to celebrate such orgies. Whether you take "tonal" or "atonal" works, it is the same picture of disintegration everywhere–inability to express an idea precisely, no matter how banal the idea may be, bad harmony and part-writing etc.

There is one composer who as early as 1910 recognized the

decline in his *Harmonielehre*[1] *(Textbook of Harmony)—* Arnold Schönberg. His new theory of "composition with twelve tones" attempts to place craftsmanship and ability on a sounder foundation, based on a new tonality which he himself created. This cannot be praised enough, for in music more than in any other art all the intellectual problems are related to the problems of the technique of the composition.

In musicology it is the same picture. A lack of new methods is felt everywhere, while in other branches of art new methods have been practised for some time. For instance, no sociology of music exists (apart from a short paper by Max Weber)[2] and even the most able thinkers who have something to say, like Paul Bekker[3] and Adolf Weissmann[4], at the most only transpose the new idealist philosophy (Husserl's Phenomenology)[5] to music. On the other hand, there is a growing habit of drawing up compendiums and fat volumes, of using muddled phraseology, blown-up with commonplaces and an incapacity to say anything that is even halfway to the point.

This bewilderment in private and public opinion, this ignorance of workmanship, this inability to achieve a more general effect is, however, in screaming contradiction to a type of music life which has assumed increasingly bigger dimensions since the war and is already making a considerable noise. For example, in Germany there are a host of modern music societies organizing a lot of concerts; to be sure they are held in half-empty halls from which the public is mostly excluded. But the big music festivals have become downright stock exchanges, where the value of the works is assessed and contracts for the coming season are settled. Yet all this noise is carried out in the vacuum of a bell glass, so to speak, so that not a sound can be heard outside. An empty officiousness celebrates orgies of inbreeding, while there is a complete lack of interest or participation of a public of any kind.

Certainly, some of the younger composers are refusing to

continue in this way. They are making every effort to be modern, more or less refusing to accept absolute music and turning their attention to the stage.

Yet when words and actions are added to their music we see all the more precisely how completely unmodern the young composers are.

For instance, recently on a German operatic stage a lot of major inventions could be seen, steam engines, automobiles, film projectors, radios and so on, which, due to their serviceability, we are assured, caused a general stir.[6]

Perhaps one shouldn't joke about it. After all, it is a step forward, and if these young composers are very assiduous, then perhaps they will one day notice that the earth is inhabited by human beings and not by stage props. If they are even more assiduous perhaps they will notice later on that these human beings are not one homogeneous mass, but are divided into classes and that they themselves are experiencing what seems to be the most gigantic social struggle in the history of mankind. Then the musician who loves his art, and for whom it is an absolute necessity, will be horrified to see how completely isolated is his art. Nevertheless, he must recognize this and not be misled by the hectic activity of an inbred music trade.

If someone comes along and says, "All right, that's quite correct, but what shall we do? Where do we go from here?" then one should not answer with frivolous optimism, "To perdition," which may sound nice but won't quite do!

Perhaps he should be given the following advice, get out of your spiritual isolation and get interested in everything, not only night life and sport, which in any case don't interest you. Never forget, machines are there solely to satisfy the needs of man. When you are composing and you open the window, remember that the noise of the street is not mere noise, but is made by man. For a time really try to do without inflated symphonic music, playful chamber music and esoteric poetry. Choose texts and subjects that concern as many people as possible.

Try to understand your own time and do not get caught up in mere formalities. Discover the people, the real people, discover day-to-day life for your art, and then perhaps you will be re-discovered.

Source: *Zur Situation der modernen Musik,* Typescript, Hanns Eisler Archives.
This article was probably written at the end of 1928. It is based on an analytical article *Über moderne Musik,* published in *Rote Fahne,* Berlin, Oct. 15, 1927.
EGW III/1, pp. 88–92.

1 The correct date of publication of *Die Harmonielehre* by Schönberg is 1911.

2 Max Weber (1864–1920), sociologist and socio-economist, established the theory of bourgeois music sociology which he set forth in his brochure *Die rationalen und soziologischen Grundlagen der Musik.*

3 Paul Bekker (1882–1937), a writer on music, one of the most influential spokesmen for *Neue Musik* in Europe. One of his publications, printed in 1919, was *Kunst und Revolution.*

4 Adolf Weissmann (1873–1929), musicologist, published a paper in 1922 entitled, *Die Musik in der Weltkrise.*

5 Edmund Husserl (1859–1938), philosopher, considered the founder of the subjective-idealist phenomenology, the Theory of Phenomena.

6 The production on a German opera stage which Eisler refers to probably was Ernst Křenek's opera *Jonny spielt auf,* 1st performance in Leipzig, Feb. 10, 1927.

Progress in the Workers'
Music Movement
1931

The workers' music movement has now entered a new phase of planned experiment. It is significant that this new and fruitful phase, which is already showing some theoretical and practical results, appears at a moment when the *Deutscher Arbeitersängerbund* (DASB–German Workers' Choral Society)[1], the chief organization of the workers' music movement, has formed a vigorous revolutionary opposition to the narrow-minded reformist leadership within its ranks.

The obstacle to progress lies mainly in the false ideas about music and the difficulty in combatting them. The anarchic bourgeois music business produces a kind of music fetishism with the result that broad masses of the people are only able to take in music in its stupidest, most dangerous, but above all its most acceptable, soporific form. Moreover, technical devices–the record player and radio– are organizing this flight from reality on a mass scale. The reformists have no desire to change things in this respect, they only endeavor to clothe the narcotic possibilities in a more noble mantle, on the principle, the farther removed from reality the nobler.

The progress achieved stems mainly from the revolutionary opposition in the DASB. A circle was formed spontaneously at the Marxist School for Workers[2] after a course on an historical-materialist approach to music, where, in addition to working-class officials a number of left-wing musicologists and music theoreticians took part, and this circle is attempting to apply the method of dialectical materialism to music. A number of specialists from the bourgeois camp have also come over to the side of the revolutionary workers. Together with Karl Rankl[3], composers and conductors like Josef Schmidt, Vladimir Vogel[4], Karl Vollmer, Ernst Hermann Meyer and others should be mentioned.

With regard to progress, experience has taught us that we must make a difference between music to listen to and music to perform. In arriving at this formulation we had to break with conventional opinions on choral singing. For us it was no longer enough for a piece to have an effect on the listeners because it was well sung by a choir: we had to find methods to revolutionize the singers as well, not to regard them simply as interpreters. We were forced to broach the question of revolutionizing the working-class singers because for years and years they of the DASB had been singing a number of revolutionary songs, yet remained reformists in political life. One contribution to a solution of this question was *Die Massnahme* (The Measures Taken).[5]

The activities of the agit-prop groups brought to light the great contradictions between the "serious" songs of choirs and the topical fighting songs. We are now trying to change the extraordinary situation in which the workers' choral movement has not produced a single fighting song for the mass movement during the last ten years. Because of this their audiences are forced into the same position as concert listeners; in the agit-prop groups it is different. Yet we are well aware that it is wrong only to listen to a fighting song; that the activating purpose of a fighting song can only be achieved if the people sing it themselves. Unemployed workers from the Fichte organization[6] spontaneously formed a small agit-prop choir and taught new fighting songs to the audiences at mass meetings.

Concerning the style of revolutionary music we formulated the following: the style, that is the method of organizing the tones, should vary according to the purpose of the music. A song of struggle to be sung by the people in the audience must be constructed differently from a choral work with a theoretical content. So our aesthetic standards are not inflexible, but when composing we take into consideration the revolutionary purpose for which we are writing.

Further experience induced us to reject the concert form. The concert form arose in the epoch of the bourgeoisie and is useless for the purposes of the revolutionary working class. It can only offer noncommitted pleasure and make the listener passive. In the next few years it will be our task to develop further the ideas of the didactic play in practical experiment.

Summarizing, we can say that all the attempts made and the progress achieved were and are only possible in close association with the militant working class. First we must never forget that those cultural organizations which sever their connections with the political organizations of the working class will necessarily become shallow and petty bourgeois.

We must not become too easy-going or be satisfied with the usual effects of music, but must aspire to something more than that, examining and improving our methods again and again so that the wonderful tasks that the class struggle places before music can be accomplished.

Source: *Fortschritte in der Arbeitermusikbewegung* in *Kampfmusik,* Berlin, 1931, No. 4.
EGW III/1, pp. 113–115.

1 *Deutscher Arbeitersängerbund* – DAS or DASB (German Workers' Choral Association) founded in 1908; main organization of the workers' music movement in Germany with nearly 315,000 members in 1932. The revolutionary choral societies, choir conductors and composers who had been expelled from the DASB by the reformist association

leaders, formed the *Kampfgemeinschaft der Arbeitersänger* (Fighting Association of Working Class Singers) in 1931. Their periodical was *Kampfmusik*.

2 The Marxist School for Workers (MASCH), established in 1926, as an educational arm of the German Communist Party, centered in Berlin. By 1931 similar institutions arose in 26 other towns. From 1928 Hanns Eisler taught at MASCH on such subjects as "Music and the Proletariat," "Music and Class Struggle," and "An Historical-materialist Approach to Music."

3 Karl Rankl (1898–1968), a gifted conductor of the left wing of the German working-class choral movement, and friend of Eisler's since their studies under Schönberg, conducted most of Eisler's compositions for working-class choirs; emigrated to England in 1933, where he died in 1968.

4 Vladimir Vogel (1896–) born in Moscow, studied in Berlin and worked there from 1924 onwards as composer and teacher of composition. Vogel's recognition of the role of the working-class music movement Eisler considered as confirmation of his theory that bourgeois music life was stagnating, and a genuine revival could only be achieved in the course of the revolutionary struggles of the working class. In 1933 Vogel was expelled from Germany; in 1935 he settled in Ascona, Switzerland. He is now counted among the leading Swiss composers.

5 *Die Massnahme* (The Measures Taken), didactic play by Brecht, music by Eisler.

6 Fichte organization was a working-class sports movement in Germany with a long tradition, with their own choirs and bands.

The Builders
of a New Music Culture
1931

To define what is new in music, with its many aspects, it is necessary to analyze the situation in music and above all to examine it critically. The difficulties of such an examination are indeed great. The division of labor on which the capitalist mode of production is founded has led to a peculiar division between specialist and amateur in art. That indicates the difficulty of talking scientifically about music. If we want to discuss art in such a way that we not only describe it, but also obtain practical and useful results then it is essential to introduce scientific methods, not only into the production of art, but also into the conception of art. There is a particular difficulty in introducing science into the sphere of music, which can only be described in explanatory terms that stem from musical technique and with which the musical amateur may not be acquainted.

If we question the average bourgeois consumer of art today about his views on music we would get the following answer: Music has existed from time immemorial and always will. It is a phenomenon above society, which of course, can also partly be explained by social situations, but which, however, assumes an independent character. Changes in art styles are explained by changes in taste. There is a certain degree of perfection in music, existing independently of man, and which will ultimately assert itself, even if it has not been observed by the people in general. For what is truly great will assert itself at some time. If mankind were to disappear the great values of music would still endure, independently following their own inherent laws, outside of and despite human society.

This conception of music as a phenomenon above society leads to the following aesthetic views: There is an imaginary harmony outside of society and independent of it, that is the musical ideal which is or is not achieved by the individual and particular work of art. The degree of perfect harmony achieved by the work of art can be determined. The methods of determining art values are partly technical and partly of a purely emotional nature. Yet these are general methods and so they may be applied by everyone, no matter to what social class he belongs.

Those are the conceptions of music and of the value of musical works which can generally be met with today, with some minor variations. How have these opinions, drawn from musical practice, affected the practice of music and vice versa? It must be confirmed that these opinions have caused further confusion, for if applied to one and the same work by various individuals, varying assessments result. Individual taste alone is the criterion, but cannot be substantiated either technically or ideologically. This widespread and still growing confusion shows that the methods in question are almost no longer applicable. One of the most obvious signs of crisis in bourgeois music is its anarchic character. The changes in musical fashion are anarchic, the concert business is anarchic, even reactions to the crisis in concert life are anarchic. The crisis in concert music has particularly sharpened in the last few years and is perhaps one of the more obvious forms of the threatening disaster, forecasting the transition from ordered bourgeois musical relations to a state of barbarism. The most plausible explanation of the crisis in concert life is a social one. Through the disappropriation of the middle class due to inflation, and the increasing proletarianization of the broad petty bourgeoisie, the prewar level of education and also the level of musical education which stabilized the practice of concert-going have been made impossible to sustain. The broad masses of the petty bourgeoisie, employees and even the middle class have become dependent upon a music that easily gratifies in a time of difficult and precarious economic conditions. We ourselves have all experienced the breakthrough of so-called light or cheerful music, formerly discounted as lacking in seriousness. Even in such places of privilege as the concert hall or the opera house, the most facile musical pleasure–jazz–has broken through. Jazz makes it possible to a high degree to entertain the listener in a most vital but noncommittal way, since it makes no demands on him at all. It is not only in jazz that the function of pure pleasure, which we described as the function of bourgeois music, becomes a pure stimulant. The *Weltanschauung* (world outlook) as a means of pleasure*, such as we find in the great era of bourgeois music, is dead. The function has become exclusively the provision of momentary stimuli. This is the only way in which the quickly changing musical fashions of the last fifteen years can be explained. The stimuli wear off very rapidly and so in the latest period of bourgeois music, where the function has remained the same, there has been a continuous need for new methods in music. These do not arise from a general change in the function of music within society, but from the urge for change while maintaining the same function–entertainment. One hundred and fifty years ago entertainment still had a committed character, for instance, a heroic character, but now entertainment has become a noncommittal device for amusement. It serves to reproduce the labor power in the capitalist meaning of the word. This process takes on barbaric forms, yet despite this, has a progressive character for the dialectical materialist. That sounds incomprehensible and so we must explain it in greater detail.

The development of music in the last fifteen years has eradicated once and for all the formerly stable bourgeois art terms concerning the personality of the artist and the independence of the work of art. The all-embracing charac-

---

* In the classical period pleasure was derived from a music which was based on a philosophy.

ter of the bourgeois music business has been destroyed and finally removed. On the ruins of this music culture room has been made for the struggle of the workers for a new music culture corresponding to their class situation which, today, is already beginning to take on a clear shape.

Music Practice and Music Consumption in Capitalism

The sharp contradiction between work and leisure peculiar to the capitalist mode of production divides all intellectual activities into those serving work and those serving leisure. Leisure, however, is a system for reproducing labor power. The content of leisure must not be the content of work. Leisure is dedicated to non-production in the interests of production. This is the socio-economic basis for the peculiar form of musical practice in capitalism.

First I must give you a short outline of the attitude to and the practice of music in feudal times in order to make clear the contrast between the musical methods of feudalism and those of the bourgeoisie. In the era of feudalism we find music in the following forms: music at the courts as a privilege of the ruling upper circles, music in the church as a means of instruction and education for the ruled class, music at work and in daily life in the form of work songs, love songs and so on. But that must not be divided rigidly. At a certain point in the development of society, church music takes over and adapts folk song, while court music uses the construction methods of church music. We must now introduce a new term into our considerations and that is the term—the function of music. By that we mean the social purpose of music-making. In feudalism the function of music for the small privileged upper class was pleasure and entertainment, for the oppressed classes it was disciplinary. Here again we must be careful not to be inflexible. Even the disciplinary function of music, for instance in military music, carries with it aspects of pleasure, but for the privileged class pleasure was its aim; that is the decisive social aspect.

For the Church Fathers music is only justified if it is compatible with Christian doctrines and enhances church services. In their judgments they are moved solely by practical considerations for the church of their time. Art as an end in itself and aesthetic pleasure only is strictly condemned. I would like to draw your attention to the last sentence, since it defines the whole content of present-day bourgeois attitudes to music. If the Church Fathers already opposed this attitude in early feudalism, it indicates that even then social contradictions existed between the strata of town burghers and the lords of the manors. The Church Fathers arrived at this radical attitude to the aesthetics of music mainly in order to achieve a clear division between church and heathen music; in the latter, chromatics especially were frowned upon as weakening and pernicious elements. In feudalism music was only allowed if it was in the service of the church, and even there it had a subordinate role compared with the word. The Church Fathers concluded that: "Music is given to man by God to facilitate the learning of psalms." The sensuous charm of music could not be eliminated, but the church sought to make it harmless by turning it into a handmaid of the church, and laid great stress only on the word and on the frame of mind of the singers, but not of the listeners. The foregoing quotation was taken from Professor Abert's book *Die Musikanschauung des Mittelalters (The Approach to Music in the Middle Ages)*. Professor Abert further shows that every kind of melodious singing and every ornamentation were strictly forbidden. "It is not seemly for the pious nor for the aged to embellish their singing or to bring forth rough tones, but they should praise God with restrained voice, so that they do not arouse the impression of music-making, but rather that of sighing." Apart from facilitating the learning of psalms and strengthening the emotional effect of the words, music had also the function of evoking and intensifying a state of repentance in the congregation. These were peculiar aesthetics accruing from the point of view of ruling class interests which, when applied in practice, further stabilized feudal relations. The Church Father Hieronymus said, and you must agree that this is a peculiar aesthetic view: "No matter how bad anybody's voice is, if his deeds are good, then before God he is an agreeable singer. Christ's servant should sing. Not the voice of the singer but his words should please." Holy Augustus warns emphatically against a too sensuous sound, for then attention would be turned away from the word of God with the danger of committing a grievous sin. The practical Church Fathers warn all their singers that their disposition and their conduct must conform to the content of what they sing, otherwise their singing will be valueless to themselves and also to the congregation. Music production in early feudalism, too, had peculiar prerequisites. Music is not a matter of ability resulting from talent, but presents itself as a sum of tenets which anyone can and must acquire. Finally, there is also the practical attitude of the composer himself which is in marked contrast to the bourgeois idea of an artist. Johannes Cottonius, a theoretician, said: "The artist should always have in mind the characteristics of the public whom he wishes to affect."

We can summarize the functions of church music, then, as follows: Music in the church is not directed towards the individual or his individual fate, but has the task of making all participants adopt a certain religious bearing. Thus, by allowing the listener to take part in the music himself later on, by joining in the chorale, he takes part in a kind of exercise and so is forced all the more effectively and firmly into a particular bearing. Pleasure in music in this case is a subordinate ingredient. This form of music-making corresponded to the class interests of the lords of the manors, the feudal lords, and in practice made feudalism possible and stabilized it again and again. Arising from this social function a certain method of constructing tones arose, which we will simply call musical technique.

The technique of composing in the Middle Ages was the following: The presentation of musical ideas was polyphonic. Pre-classical polyphony knows of no contrasts, either in the tempo or in the formal arrangement. One of the specific features of this technique is the lack of variation, that is of the variation of a subject, which makes possible its thematic development. The musical subject is not changed by division, by repetition or by driving it forward, not developed as in the classical music of the nineteenth century. The musical development is accomplished through additions in the other voices. This, generally speaking, is the essence of polyphonic presentation, for a canon, or imitation, is no more than bringing development into a static musical idea by singing or playing it at different levels, at different pitches and at different times.

The instrumentation is not instrumentation in a bourgeois sense. It is pure construction of parts without color and without effects. The rendition is carried out with a certain uniform tone. Crescendi and decrescendi are missing. There is a lack of modulation. We can see from this how a certain social situation leads to a certain musical technique which, in turn, when applied in practice makes this particular social situation possible.

The bourgeoisie, still in the lap of feudalism, is in opposition to the feudal methods of production. Now first I must explain this social contradiction in the economic sphere, so that we can make it clear in such a difficult domain as music. One of these contradictions was that between manufacture and ground rent. The profit from feudal ground rent springs from a peculiar social structure, that of serfdom. But what are the historical prerequisites for the existence of capital? As Marx wrote: "The historical prerequisites for the coming into being of capital are first the accumulation of a certain sum of money in the hands of individual persons when, on the whole, there is a relatively high standard of commodity production and secondly the existence of 'free' workers in a twofold sense," that is free of all restrictions or limitations in the sale of his labor power, and free of landed property and of the means of production altogether. As Marx ironically calls him, a worker "free as a bird."*

This economic contradiction leads to a political struggle of the young bourgeoisie against serfdom. It leads to the discovery of human rights.

Another economic contradiction under feudalism, for example, was the one between free trade and the feudal privilege over landed property. In this connection I would like to allude to an early article by Kautsky[1]–from the good time of his youth–today he is greatly changed. It concerns the transport of a cask of wine from Amiens to Paris to be traded. For instance, this cask of wine costs the sum of 20 francs in Amiens. In Paris, however, it costs 50 francs, for the cart carrying the cask of wine has to pass along many roads over which the feudal lords had so-called toll rights. The feudal lord could, without capital investment, make a profit through the inherited privilege of his class, merely by exacting a toll on the roads. In feudal opinion these privileges were ordained by God. Opposed to them was the idea of liberty which the young men of enterprise had. This economic idea of freedom also corresponds to a political conception of freedom as expressed in the rights of man in the French Revolution: the purpose of every social order is the maintenance of the three natural and unwritten human rights. These three rights are freedom, property and security, and resistance to tyranny. Here we have a classic example of how economic interests take on political forms and how political forms finally take on an inflexible character in *Weltanschauung*. These general theories are only general insofar as they make possible in general the capitalist mode of production, but how were they applied in practice? The right to resistance against tyranny was dropped very soon. Only the right to property was

---

* This is a play on words meaning "outlawed."

43

retained and that meant private property in the bourgeois sense. Today as well, that is in 1931, this economic idea of freedom of the men of enterprise still corresponds to a political conception of freedom as found, for instance, in the Weimar Constitution. There it says, for example: "The dwelling of every German is a refuge and is inviolable." However, we have to add that one must first have and pay for a dwelling, so that it can be a refuge and inviolable, and that one may not have committed any political offence to be presented with a house search warrant. Then it says further in the Weimar Constitution: "Every German has the right to acquire a plot of land," whereby I must add that 99 percent of the German people are hardly in a position to make use of this peculiar right, since the small change necessary to exercise this right is lacking. This conception of freedom, dictated by economic interests and applied in practice, again makes possible certain economic relations. It is also the basis of bourgeois art production, art practice and thus, of course, of bourgeois music. The great musical struggles under feudalism started under the banner of the "struggle for true music," reflecting the fierce struggle of the bourgeoisie against feudalism. At the beginning of this struggle the bourgeoisie is in direct opposition to the church and thus also to the feudal function of music. The feudal function of music made possible the social purpose of evoking and intensifying in the congregation a state of repentance, but the new function in bourgeois society is that of allowing a harmonious development of the individual personality and is directly opposed to the feudal function.

To describe bourgeois music as graphically as possible, we must say that the term "commodity" which is indeed the decisive factor in capitalism, has spread into the realm of music. The concert form signifies the introduction of commodity relations into music. Concert ticket-buying, the sale of sheet music, the term music specialist—the producers of music commodities—are all characteristic of this.

44

The classical concert music of the bourgeoisie is aimed at the buyer of music commodities and endeavors to entertain him. It is clear that in a social situation proclaiming itself to be the proof of the freedom of the individual, that is, the freedom of the entrepreneur and the free play of economic forces, there is no longer any natural function for music as it existed under feudalism. Yet this concert form, apparently in gross contradiction to the feudal privilege of entertainment music, proves on closer examination to be merely a more democratic form of the privilege of property. For while a church concert could plainly be heard by the feudal listeners, in the concert form of the bourgeoisie a peculiar prerequisite for the enjoyment of music appears on the scene. It is the condition of education and elementary musical education. For bourgeois music is not universal music either, but likewise the art of a ruling class. The bigger the contrast between bourgeoisie and proletariat becomes, the bigger the distinctive contrast in music becomes, and this to its full extent only under capitalism. This contrast is commonly characterized as the difference between easy and difficult music. It is also claimed that there is serious and non-serious music, or serious and light music. But all these labels cannot hide the fact that this contradiction has arisen from a social contradiction. Church music, once the standard-bearer of the whole of musical development, is being pushed into the background. It is no longer the socially decisive factor. Its technical development is drawn from concert music and thus also changes its feudal function. The burgher is also a churchgoer, for he has long since buried the hatchet against the church, and now makes use of church ideology against the working class, in the same way as feudalism once used it against the bourgeoisie. This bourgeois function of pleasure, of the harmonious development and upholding of the individual personality, led to the great development of homophonic music in the nineteenth century. The early revolutionary individual is reflected in the beginnings of this

45

bourgeois music development, which we must place at about the middle of the eighteenth century with the Mannheim School. The greatest heights of bourgeois music were reached in Beethoven's symphonies in which the pleasure was re-functioned to become a kind of philosophical world outlook. While at revolutionary periods revolutionary bourgeois music reflects the great revolutionary individual in his actual struggle against feudalism, by the middle of the nineteenth century it also reflects the disappointed, property-preserving petty bourgeoisie. The great emotions became poorer, petty, they became more intimate. The decline of the bourgeois class, its militant attitude towards the rising proletariat made pleasure become more and more of an end in itself, more and more problematic and debased. Contemporary bourgeois artists in prominent positions in the end became wildly egocentric as a matter of course, only producing commodities for a small élite and in extreme cases for the production of a commodity only.

This peculiar function of bourgeois music corresponds to a peculiar technique of composition–homophony. It is the manner of presenting the musical ideas of bourgeois classical music. It is built on the principle of contrast first and foremost. This principle guarantees to a high degree variety and entertainment. The development of harmony and its theoretical derivations make possible ever more new methods of contrast. Finally, contrast is also guaranteed by the technique of instrumentation, which introduces timbre as a musical means of presentation. The rendering becomes alive, subtle gradations of crescendi and decrescendi are discovered. This style is appropriate, as no other, for appealing to the individual experience and to the individual imagination. The listener is not forced to take a predetermined attitude but an attempt is made to excite him, to entertain him and to create associations for him.

This process of development is to be found in all other arts. It is also to be found in science. The best example of a similar development, like that of church music to concert music, is the development of the scholastic philosophy of the Middle Ages to the Encyclopedists of the eighteenth century and modern bourgeois philosophy. In bourgeois music at the beginning of the nineteenth century there was still something of an all-embracing attitude, a sort of musical world outlook, yet at the end of the nineteenth century the acute crisis in bourgeois music coincided with the beginnings of the crisis in capitalism. The extraordinary sharpness of this crisis was prophesied and described by Marx eighty years ago, as a crisis of all nations, and that is what we are experiencing today.

In order to depict the anarchy in bourgeois music we must make clear the different trends, which in addition, are engaged in bitter combat with each other. The right wing of the music movement in Germany, roughly represented by the periodical *Zeitschrift für Musik* in Leipzig founded by Robert Schumann, represents the period from Wagner to Richard Strauss. They are the last, rather weak fighters for the all-embracing character of bourgeois music, which is practically finished. They oppose *Gebrauchsmusik*[2], they are for soul-searing and soul-enrichment of the individual, for symphonies with a world outlook and for symphonic poems. They reject the technical progress of the left wing and believe that the values of a certain short historical epoch are eternal. Politically they also yearn for a more powerful, imperialist prewar Germany, possibly under the leadership of the Hohenzollerns. They are in favor of concerts; they would like to revive the musical situation of 1880–1914. The purely professional level of this right wing is very low. In the main they have antiquated notions concerning music and have no ties with the broader petty-bourgeois masses. This last position, despite the actual crisis, presents the illusion of a stable musical situation. It is a parody of the attitude of bourgeois music at the end of the nineteenth century which, after all, was still productive. One of their most able thinkers, Heinrich Schenker[3], has even gone into opposition, because he only approves of music up to Schubert. To prove how political this right wing is on questions of music (so not only we cursed dialectical materialists are so confoundedly political) I quote from Schenker's book *Neue musikalische Theorien* (New Musical Theories): "The world war ended with Germany unconquered in the field, but betrayed by the democratic parties, the parties of the mediocre and worse, of the unbridled individualism of semi-literates and illiterates, of incompetency to synthesize, of know-all and really knowing nothing, of irresponsible doctrinairism and of bloodthirsty experimentation, combined with terror, mass murder, forgery, lies about the people, idolizing and imitating the West etc., who have taken over from the hostile Western peoples the lie of their form of freedom. Thus the last bulwark of the aristocratism has fallen and nature sees itself betrayed to democracy—fundamentally and organically inimical to nature. For culture is selective, the profoundest synthesis on the basis of the miraculous achievements of genius."

This right wing, which of course contains diverse shades and opinions, is conducting a hopeless struggle to maintain and propagate bourgeois music of the nineteenth century. In principle, they oppose every innovation.

The center of the bourgeois music front is represented roughly by journals such as *Musikblätter des Anbruch*, or the music columns of dailies like the *Frankfurter Zeitung* or the *Berliner Tageblatt*. Politically they correspond roughly to party groupings from the *Deutsche Staatspartei*[4] to the *Deutsche Volkspartei*[5] or the *Zentrum Partei*[6]. This group, too, sighs for the good old times, but is not blind to reality. It sees the crisis and tries to combine in some measure tradition and progress. It is for Beethoven and school music. It is in favor of including the exotic, it might even approve Arnold Schönberg, and it is also for the workers' music movement in a modified form. It expects everything to emanate from the creative power of individual geniuses and the high quality of their works. This group has also adopted Schenker's opinion that culture is selective, the profoundest synthesis on the basis of the miraculous achievements of genius. But this group admits of development and above all favors the riches of music. In the opinion of representatives of this trend what is really good will always find a place, and good modern music will join it. What is good is simply good! The theoretical vanguard of this group do not ask themselves from where they take their values, nor do they ask about music's function in society.

The left wing of the bourgeois music movement is the most interesting. It is the most sensitive and quickest to react to reality. It is highly versatile, and is represented by the journal *Melos*, and by composers like Stravinsky and Hindemith. You could almost say, it is the vanguard of bourgeois music in collapse, and technically the most progressive wing. A composer like Arnold Schönberg must also be counted among this group. This wing has shown an extremely lively reaction to the crisis in concert life. Since reality eradicated the musical function of *Weltanschauung* as a means of pleasure, this group went one step further. They said music should not reflect the world outlook—actually a progressive idea of the bourgeoisie—and discovered the terms *Spielfreude*[7] and *Gebrauchsmusik*. In this way noncommitted amusement was counted as progress and became acceptable. Music should be a mere play on tones, not expressing any human feelings. A new virtuosity appeared, a new spirituality, a new elegance and a new noncommittal gaiety. Music must be so constructed to avoid expressing anything pathetic, banal or magnanimous. Ideally it should be refrigerated, should not stir the inner emotions of the listeners. It is best of all, as Stravinsky said years ago, if it runs like a sewing machine. In the last two years this left wing has executed a huge turnabout under the pressure of the acute crisis in Germany and has once again discovered the soul and a new lyricism.

In Berlin Paul Hindemith, the avant-garde exponent of *Spielfreude,* recently experienced the first performance of his oratorio *Das Unaufhörliche* (The Unceasing). This oratorio is a curious work, for it shows that in the search for new stimuli the bourgeoisie is returning to their world outlook at the time of their deepest crisis. In the search for new stimuli in a decadent period the world outlook is brought forward again. And so the circle of Schenker and the *Neue Zeitschrift für Musik* to Stravinsky, Hindemith and the *Berliner Tageblatt* has closed ranks to become one front. But on the way to this united front of the bourgeoisie in music something got lost and was destroyed once and for all. In the past the bourgeois artist reflected a full and whole personality. At the present time our music personalities such as Stravinsky and Hindemith are very undecided as to how they should compose. Almost every work or group of works by Stravinsky is in a different style. The modern bourgeois artist is tottering like the foundations of the bourgeois order. And so the latest achievement, the united front of bourgeois music is a tottering unity only.

These three groups of what is really the big bourgeois music movement confront the folk music movement under the leadership of Jöde[8] and the musical activities of the Social Democrats. In practice they are concerned mainly with the cultivation of old church music and folk songs. It also has real political motivations. I would like to quote only one sentence of Jöde's which has taken effect: "Turn youth away from politics through the revival of folk songs." The reformist music activities of the Social Democrats are merely a feeble copy of the bourgeois-democratic center group. They are advocates of concert music and Jöde, of Stravinsky and Richard Strauss. In fact, they advocate everything. They think much will emerge from some kind of mystic effect of music. The most significant advice of the consultant to the Ministry, Professor Kestenberg[9], is that the worker must free himself through "singing air!" In this reformist workers' music movement there is a left wing—an opposition formed by the revolutionary workers. Recently, however, some of them have been expelled from the big music organizations of the working class, for instance, from the DASB, the German Workers' Choral Society. The reformists maintain that they were not expelled for political but for formal reasons. The opposition was supposed to have violated a statute at some time, which provided the opportunity to throw the liveliest and most progressive sections of the workers' music movement out of their own organizations.

What are the prospects for music, in which class will new methods be created, which class will build a new relation between life and art, between practice and theory? Which class, due to its economic situation, has an urgent interest in a new function of music? A new music cannot arise through material revolution, but only through social changes in which a new class takes power, and in which art also has a new social function. The application of scientific methods gives an answer to this question. The only class which needs new methods and for whom a change in the function of music is a vital necessity is the revolutionary proletariat. In the process of their struggle for power and for building socialism they will find new methods in the course of practice—some have already been found. They already contain in embryo the first bases of the methods for a socialist music culture. In order fully to understand this development a short outline of the history of the workers' music movement is called for.

The Workers' Music Movement

The first stage of music-making among the workers is remarkable not for its "high" cultural level compared perhaps with that of the bourgeoisie, but for their original use of music. Certainly, the form of the music societies was taken over from the bourgeoisie, but the first music associations of working people show essential differences from bourgeois organizations. The main difference is that the first workers' choral societies which arose in Germany roughly around 1860–70 had a real political task. At the time of the illegal political struggle under the anti-socialist laws, they were a cloak for political activity. It is indicative of the militant character of an apparently purely cultural organization that immediately after their foundation they were put under police surveillance and finally suppressed. That teaches us the classical attitude of the proletariat to culture. Under compulsion to reproduce labor power through leisure–here through musical activity–these cultural organizations are immediately forced into the class situation of the workers and take on a militant character. Precisely this makes it impossible for them to confine themselves exclusively to bourgeois *Liedertafel* literature (glees), which only depicts the relation of the individual to nature, love, *Gemütlichkeit,* conviviality. The obligation to defend their organization entails attack which in cultural matters is agitation and propaganda; this finally leads to the birth of a distinctive form of music, *Tendenzlied.*

Workers were not yet in a position to be culturally effective themselves, due to their one-sided employment in the production process. At that time they did not establish a new musical direction, but they did introduce a new method. With regard to their musical material, that is to say from the bourgeois aesthetic standpoint, it was a style which was regarded as old-fashioned and ridiculous by the more advanced circles of the bourgeoisie. If anyone had said in 1880 that these somewhat clumsy, blatantly red songs of the workers were the means by which they would possess the great heritage of German classical music, it would have seemed utter rubbish even to the most discerning mind. Yet it is correct, for history has taught us that every new musical style has not arisen from an aesthetically new point of view and therefore does not represent a material revolution, but the change in the material is conditioned as a matter of course by an historically necessary change in the function of music in society as a whole.

We must also discover this ever-recurring process in the beginnings of the workers' music movement. Only aesthetically dimmed eyes and dialectically unschooled heads can fail to appreciate these small signs of a change in function. This change in function was of necessity small, since it was conditional upon the distinctive situation of the class-conscious workers at the end of the nineteenth century. While science was executing only propagandistic exercises, while social pressure and unmitigated capitalism were making the broad masses ripe for Marxism, it stands to reason that the art of the workers was not yet able to reflect progressive ideas. At that time *Tendenzkunst* was an art which the class-conscious worker offered to the non-class-conscious worker with the object of stirring both of them, of arousing class instincts and of drawing him into the class struggle. Music and text, therefore, had to appeal to the non-class-conscious worker and to the emotions of the individual and were actually only the preliminary to a planned propaganda action.

In the years between 1880 and 1914 a large number of such works appeared in vocal literature which, aesthetically judged, meant adopting the backward music style of the bourgeoisie. Today we know that this was an historical condition, since the education that the bourgeoisie provides for the modern industrial proletarian fits him only for exploitation, and fails to equip him with what the bourgeois artist calls a profound appreciation of art. The musical material offered to both singers and listeners thus had to be quite simple and so constructed to guarantee a purely emotional effect in the listeners. In addition to this purely practical artistic activity of the workers we must examine yet another aspiration.

It is the old idea of national education which, when applied in the musical field, means the music of feudalism and of the bourgeoisie to be taken over by the workers. Right from the beginning it was love's labor's lost, for the economic situation of the working class makes it impossible for them to take the same attitude to art as the bourgéoisie. This is the old classical mistake of every reformist action, which leads as a matter of course to compromise and which necessarily results in aesthetically valuable material being played off against politically valuable material, and which unknowingly, furthers the aims of the bourgeoisie.

It is clear that we must combat these reformist aspirations as well. However, the workers are not only threatened by this danger, they are also threatened by the vulgar petty-bourgeois view of art, which infiltrates into the working class from sections of the bourgeoisie. We must remember that the operetta, the hit song, false and genuine folk songs are listened to by a large proportion of all strata of society and that the workers are faced here with just as big a danger as musical snobbism. The cultivation of classical music is correct if it is used to liquidate light entertainment music. The advantages of classical music over entertainment music are clear, in that a certain demand is made of working-class listeners to be atttentive, while entertainment music makes no such demand and rather panders to laziness and comfort. It is important to counter this danger for working-class listeners by performing the great works of bourgeois music. Yet this advantage can quickly turn into the most serious disadvantage, if it results in their taking a negative attitude towards the revolutionary movement of *Tendenzmusik*.

In order to raise the workers' music movement to the level of thought in the political struggles, it is necessary to criticize the forms of bourgeois music activities, and not to use them uncritically any longer. In addition the new social situation of the workers should be analyzed.

The old *Tendenzmusik* had the task of winning the non-class-conscious worker through the class-conscious worker. But the present-day political situation is different. The broad masses of the workers have their organizations, the trade unions, the parties, cultural and sport associations. These bodies are conducting a constant struggle to determine the correct revolutionary position. The question of tactics has become the topical question for the working class. Only when this question becomes superfluous, that is when the right tactics are adopted, will the revolution be triumphant. *Tendenzkunst* which mechanically copies the attitude of the workers' music movement of 1880, even though it includes aesthetically progressive elements, is nevertheless pointless and counterrevolutionary. In the long run it will be retrogressive, because it ignores all the contradictions in the working-class movement. It surely cannot be the task of *Tendenzmusik* to stir the emotions of the militant workers aimlessly. This would not change the situation at all. This kind of music must be superseded by a revolutionary art whose main character is militant and educative. That involves thinking about the dialectical-materialist method of thought and its results over the past eighty years; it means thinking about the revolutionary experiences of the last twenty years.

In a society where the broad masses are indeed united in the necessity for class struggle, but disunited in how it should be conducted, by what methods and with what means, art for the first time can become the great tutor of society. Art will have to depict the theory and experiences of the class struggle in powerful images. The main purpose of bourgeois art is pleasure. The working class has entered one of the most complicated and difficult periods of its class history; contradictions are rife in its own ranks. Nevertheless, it is faced with the real task of taking power and it again elects the arts as its great ally, the arts whose function is changing. Pleasure which was the main purpose becomes a means to an end. Art no longer sets out to satisfy the people's hunger for beauty, but makes use of beauty to teach the individual, to make the ideas of the working class and the actual problems of the class struggle comprehensible and attainable.

Music no longer prostitutes its beauty, but brings order and discipline into the confused emotions of each individual. We can see that a new and great change will result in the function of art. Brought forth as a teacher, as a weapon in the most difficult situation in class history, art loses all that the bourgeois artist calls "beautiful." The new function of art in a classless society is already contained to a marked degree in its beginnings.

With regard to the new methods now practised in the workers' music movement, I would like to remark: No recipe can be given here. It is the task of the specialists and experts in the workers' music movement to examine the material changes involved in the new functions of revolutionary art. At the same time the broad masses of the workers and their officials must force their experts to undertake this analysis and to control and critically examine the results by applying them in practice.

To conclude I would like to say: Socialism means the entry of reason in society. If we, and by we I mean the vanguard of the proletariat, the revolutionary workers, really want to take political power and not merely talk about it as a vague and distant hope, then we must propagate the practice of an art which takes its new methods from the daily struggles of the revolutionary workers. However, it should not only reflect their sufferings and cares, as the reformists and "social" artists believe it should, but it must clarify the right methods for taking power by the broad masses of the hungry and impoverished in Germany. Seventy years ago, in the early period of capitalism, when the German worker was still in a state of destitution and without culture, one of the classical authors of dialectical materialism, Frederick Engels, pronounced that precisely this wretched class of men and women, living under barbaric conditions, would be the only class called upon to take over the heritage of classical philosophy in Germany. This sent all the professors of the day into fits of laughter. And so I would also like to apply Engels' prediction to music and maintain that the workers, and by that I mean the Ruhr miners here in Düsseldorf, the metal workers of Solingen, the chemical proletarians of Höchst, are the only class which will eagerly take over the heritage of great bourgeois music, after the downfall and decay of the music culture of the bourgeoisie, which we are at present witnessing. From this class will emerge the builders of the new music culture of socialism.

To the progressive bourgeois musicians let it be said that the new methods of music will only emerge in the daily struggle of the revolutionary workers against the bourgeoisie; and a new music culture will only arise after the workers in Germany have taken power during the construction and completion of socialism.

Source: *Die Erbauer einer neuen Musikkultur* in Hanns Eisler, *Reden und Aufsätze,* Winfried Höntsch, ed., Leipzig, 1961, pp. 25–52.
This was a lecture given by Eisler in Düsseldorf, December 1931, where the workers' choirs were rehearsing the didactic play, *The Measures Taken* (Brecht/Eisler). The lecture was published in a slightly altered version with Eisler's agreement.
The complete text in EGW III/1, pp. 140–63.

1   Karl Kautsky (1854–1938), one of the theoreticians of the German Social Democrats, turned away from Marxism and repudiated the idea of the dictatorship of the proletariat. He was criticized by Lenin for his counterrevolutionary opinions.

2   *Gebrauchsmusik* (utility music)–term used in the twenties to denote music which was not played purely in concerts but served specific use–music for theater or film, social occasions etc.

3 Heinrich Schenker, *Neue musikalische Theorien und Phantasien*, 2nd vol., Vienna/Leipzig, 1922.

4 *Deutsche Staatspartei* (German State Party), formed in 1930 by important parts of the *Deutsche Demokratische Partei* and reactionary groups. Almost wiped out at 1932 elections.

5 *Deutsche Volkspartei* (German People's Party), bourgeois party, 1918–33 (supported by heavy industry and finance); 1920–21 and 1922–30 government party; best-known leader Gustav Stresemann.

6 *Zentrum Partei* (Center Party), leading bourgeois Catholic party founded in 1871.

7 *Spielfreude, Spielmusik*–terms allude to a certain type of music of the twenties and thirties (Hindemith, Butting etc.) which Eisler considered as too "playful" and "motoric."

8 Fritz Jöde (1887–1970), an important representative of the bourgeois music movement among the youth in Germany. Despite his doubtless worthy efforts to keep alive the traditions of folk music and customs among the youth, he was attacked by the revolutionary working-class musicians for his petty-bourgeois view of folk music and his non-involvement in the social struggles of the time.

9 Leo Kestenberg (1882–1962), pianist and music teacher, worked in the Prussian Ministry of Culture as adviser on music affairs 1919–32; supporter of a bourgeois-democratic, all-round music education; forced to emigrate in 1933.

Our Revolutionary Music

1932

Music, like every other art has to fulfill a certain purpose in society. It is used by bourgeois society mainly as recreation, for the reproduction (re-creation) of labor power, to lull people and to blunt their intellect.

The workers' music movement must be clear about the new function of their music, which is to activate their members for struggle and to encourage political education. This means that all music forms and techniques must be developed to suit the express purpose, that is the class struggle. In practice that will not result in what the bourgeoisie calls style. A bourgeois composer with "style" will solve all his musical tasks in a similar way, so that in bourgeois aesthetics they talk about an "artistic personality." In the workers' music movement we do not aspire to "style" but to new methods of musical technique, which will make it possible to use music in the class struggle better and more intensively.

The best way of describing bourgeois music is by using the term "mood," for it signifies that bourgeois music wants to "entertain" the listener. The task of workers' music will be to remove the sentimentality and pompousness from music, since these sensations divert us from the class struggle.

The most important requisite of revolutionary music is to divide it into music for practical performance: songs of struggle, satirical songs and so on, and music to be listened to: didactic plays, choral montage and choral pieces with a theoretical content.

The first requirement the class struggle places on the

mass fighting song is that it is quickly taken in, that it is easily understood, vigorous and accurate in attitude. And here lies a great danger for the revolutionary composer. Comprehensibility in bourgeois music is to be found solely in the field of popular song, and unfortunately, the mistake is often made of settling for a so-called "red" popular song. Yet the bourgeois song hit has a corrupt musical passivity which we cannot adopt. The melodic line and the harmony of the popular song are of no use. But it is possible to remould the rhythm of jazz to make it taut and vigorous.

Music to be listened to does not need the same comprehensibility as do mass fighting songs. The construction depends on the content of each piece making it possible to develop bigger and more exacting musical forms. However, the revolutionary composer can fall into other traps. First of aridity and boredom, but secondly the danger of wildly rehashing the antiquated, formal experiments of bourgeois music in the early postwar years. The music for choirs and didactic plays will have to be given a sharp and cold basic tenor, for that is how the choir must sing in expounding political slogans or theories before mass audiences.

In recent years a number of new revolutionary composers have been working actively in the workers' music movement–Vogel, Szabó[1], Vollmer, Ernst H. Meyer, Schröder, Nöthling and others. The choral montage of the Workers' Choir of Greater Berlin must be mentioned as a special achievement. Together with their conductor, Goldstein, they have proved that a choir can create a choral work for itself, if it is sufficiently eager and active politically.

Source: *Unsere Kampfmusik* in *Illustrierte Rote Post,* Berlin, March 1932, No. 11.
EGW III/1, pp. 169-70.

Blast-Furnace Music
*Work on a Sound Film in
the Soviet Union*
1932

The work on a sound film in the Soviet Union was one of
the most interesting jobs I ever tackled. In composing music
to a revolutionary film the composer is faced with new
and difficult problems, especially when the film deals with
such an important theme as youth constructing socialism.

In the sound film *Komsomol*[1] (subtitled, *Song of Heroes*),
the scene is laid in three places: in the new industrial town
of Magnitogorsk[2], in the Kuznetsk Basin, a coal mining
center and in factories in Moscow and Leningrad. I knew
at once that I would not be able to write this music without
first being on the scene. So my first job was not that of a
composer but more like that of a "music reporter." For in
fact I went with the tape recorder to Magnitogorsk, where
Joris Ivens, the Dutch director and I studied the most
important locality of the film. First, I had to know something about the work of constructing the furnaces and its
problems. Secondly, I had to record the original music of
the national minorities and the industrial noises.

Magnitogorsk is the most interesting place I have ever
visited. This town is in a permanent state of growth and
change. It is only two and a half years old and already has
275,000 inhabitants, whose work is concentrated wholly on
erecting a gigantic foundry combine for producing steel.
Practically every nationality is taking part in the erection
of this great project. Next to a Kirgizian, who two years
ago was a nomad trapper, you find a skilled German
worker; next to a young Russian construction engineer, the
new type from the working class, a highly qualified American specialist is working.

The work there was not so easy, since I am not used to clambering around in overalls on a big blast furnace looking for the most suitable place for a microphone, in order to get the best recording of the deafening roar of molten steel being cast. But the fantastic enthusiasm of Joris Ivens and the comradely help of the Komsomol organization were catching. Even today I am proud of the fact that I recorded over 750 meters of factory noises and music in seven days, in a climate to which I was unaccustomed and under great physical exertion. Recording with some old Kazakhs was especially exciting. The funny thing was that I was chasing after old folk songs while the Kazakhs wanted to sing the *Internationale* in Kazakh language for me. I was inspired by the colossal enthusiasm and spirit of the workers of all nationalities and by the sense of duty and responsibility of the Communist officials.

The second stage of my work was in Moscow, where I composed the music to the film and recorded it in the Mezhrabpom Film studios. The first piece I wrote was the Magnitogorsk Ballad of the Komsomols, together with Comrade Tretyakov[3]. The text is quite simple:

Ural, Ural,
The town by the magnetic mountain.
Here lies a lot of steel.
The Party says
Give us steel!
The Komsomols answer:
In the time planned
We will give you steel!

In the film there is a scene where a young kolkhoz farmer comes to Magnitogorsk, reports to the labor office and then walks through the town to his lodgings filled with amazement. This scene gave me the opportunity of mounting a grand orchestral piece to make clear to the audience the fundamental importance of this incident. For the distinguishing feature of Magnitogorsk is not the blast furnace alone, but the people who are transforming the steppes and erecting a great complex which, in turn, transforms its builders. A new type of man is emerging in the process.

During the shooting in the studios in Moscow I was impressed with the exemplary discipline of the technical personnel, the musicians and their class-conscious eagerness to work. You can sense something of the new type of man who knows what he is working for. The whole Joris Ivens unit was honored with the title of *Udarniki*-Brigade (Shock Brigade)[4]. I believe that this film will be an important weapon in our struggle in Germany also, and perhaps contribute to the development of revolutionary film art.

Source: *Hochofen-Musik* in *Illustrierte Rote Post*, Berlin, April 1932, No. 15.
EGW III/1, pp. 171–72.

1   In May 1932 Eisler traveled to the Soviet Union for the second time. With the film *Komsomol* or *Song of Heroes* began the cooperation between Eisler and Joris Ivens.

2   During the First Five Year Plan extensive open-cast mining began in the Southern Urals at the foot of the Magnetic Mountain. Here high quality iron ore had been found. The socialist city of Magnitogorsk arose around the metallurgical foundry combine. The coal and coke necessary for the foundry work came from the "Kusbass"–the Kuznetsk basin.

3   Sergei Tretyakov (1892–1939), writer, became acquainted with Eisler when he visited Berlin in 1931. They both intended to follow up the "Magnitnaya" subject as an opera for the Moscow Bolshoi Theater.

4   *Udarnik* is the Russian term for an activist worker. Eisler also wrote an *Udarniki* canon at this time.

Music for Workers' Orchestras
1932/33

Workers' orchestras in Germany are preoccupied with the following questions: Should they play bourgeois music? Why is there no proletarian orchestral music like the Egmont Overture[1], for example?

Should they try to play intricate modern orchestral works or should they be content to play revolutionary songs and marches? What is the difference between a revolutionary and a non-revolutionary workers' orchestra? Is it in the fact that one or more fighting songs are added to the customary program? A working-class musician can only give a revolutionary answer to this and to similar questions if he is clear about the material productive forces of music in capitalism and the way they develop. We must learn to recognize an increasing process of rationalization in music development, both in the production of music and in its reproduction. The radio, records, sound film and juke box can make the best music available to enormous numbers of people, or as is the case with gramophone records they can be retailed in canned form as commodities. The result of this rationalization process is that music production is restricted to a group of specialists which is becoming smaller, but more highly qualified. The crisis in the concert business is the crisis in the form of production which through new technical discoveries has become obsolete and outmoded. The growing unemployment among professional musicians indicates that through the property relations typical of capitalism, social progress turns into a disadvantage for those employed in the production process.

However, through the development of the forces of production, possibilities of musical enjoyment at a low cost are growing to an extent previously unknown. The working-class musician is rarely a qualified instrumentalist, due to lack of time and money, and for want of musical training. It will be hard for him to buy an instrument, and also to learn to play it tolerably well. Quite apart from the level of his ability he must learn to understand that classical as well as modern bourgeois music demands technique which even a bourgeois dilettante cannot cope with although he has more time and money at his disposal. Two hundred years ago the producer and consumer represented a progressive development in bourgeois music. The difference between amateur and professional is never so marked in primitive society, for instance among primitive tribes or in a barter economy, as it is in capitalism.

Why do workers make music? Because it gives them pleasure. The difficulties they encounter in satisfying their need for music indicate the contradiction between their leanings and their social position. A piece of classical music can only be understood if the performance does not distort it. Of course there are other preliminary conditions for understanding, such as general education, habit and practice in youth, the possession of time and money, feeling and perception.

All these things are conditions and qualities more likely to be found among bourgeois music lovers than among proletarians. The bourgeois form of musical enjoyment naturally implies a bourgeois way of life. Should working-class musicians practise bourgeois music at their rehearsals? Only a fool would answer this question with "No." It is always good to learn and study. But it is a different matter if a workers' orchestra gives a concert. With every concert the organization assumes the same responsibility for content and quality as a political speaker does for his speech. A distorted and indifferent performance of classical music does not serve the listener and gives him a false impression. The good attendance at such workers' concerts proves at best the class solidarity and the absolutely correct instinct with which the workers support their cultural organizations. But nevertheless a demonstration of solidarity should not be regarded as the sole criterion of success, but should act as an impetus to learn and develop in a revolutionary way.

The workers' orchestras could now justifiably ask, "What shall we play at our concerts then?" The answer is that a concert consisting only of orchestral works is not right for a proletarian audience. One must guard against overestimating orchestral music and considering it the only sophisticated art. Music without words first achieved its great significance and became fully developed under capitalism. So-called symphonic music is the typical bourgeois form of music-making and for this reason is not easily accessible to workers either materially or ideologically. The problem of symphonic orchestral music of a proletarian character is just as insoluble as the attempt to change a dress suit into overalls by painting it red. The bourgeois form of music-making is transitory and if the working-class musician draws practical conclusions from this knowledge he will help prepare the ground for the practice of music in a revolutionary manner.

It is necessary to do the following: every workers' orchestra should try to form a small choir with which it can rehearse fighting songs. If it is decided to give a performance, the political purpose to be served must be the first consideration and a basic idea must be agreed on depending on the requirements. For example, if the basic idea is to be "solidarity," then the orchestral committee and the choir should choose old and new fighting songs from their repertoire which are germane to this subject. After that an official representative should confer with the revolutionary writers, agit-prop groups, workers' photography circles and the Marxist Workers' School, explaining the purpose of the performance. The Marxist Workers' School should be asked to provide a speaker; and a small working team consisting of representatives from the orchestra, the choir,

66

the writers, the agit-prop group and the photography circle should work out a program. This should consist of a loose sequence of scenes, fighting songs, choral and orchestral pieces, 16 mm films and projected documentary photos. This production should be mounted partly from already existing material (and therefore it is called choral montage in Germany). The interpolated texts and individual numbers should be specially written. The specialist group for this performance should be the orchestra, taking over the responsibility for the music section: the fighting songs with choir (they should also be practised with the public), short orchestral pieces, the accompaniment to film, acting and projected documentary shots.

In such a way the workers' orchestras can offer first-class performances, since our new revolutionary style of music enables novel and original compositions to be so contrived that they can also be well executed by untrained amateurs. One can go still further by taking into consideration in the composition itself the peculiarities, the merits and weaknesses of the individual societies. Working-class musicians must demand this of their revolutionary composers, for they too, must show through their work that they are prepared to learn and that revolutionary music is not merely empty and useless talk. The reason for this kind of performance is: a workers' orchestra alone is hardly in a position to achieve anything useful; an agit-prop group or a choral society is technically too one-sided to fill a whole evening's program. Yet if all these cultural organizations which are at present isolated cooperate they will be able to supplement each other. This cooperation will prepare the technical conditions for large-scale meetings where political subjects furthering the revolution bring the message to the masses of the people in an original and artistically effective manner. This means breaking with many cherished opinions and habits; it means a lot of trouble and discomfort and it means not being deterred by difficulties and failures. Working-class musicians who choose this path will certainly act in a true revolutionary manner, for they will lay the first foundations of a new revolutionary workers' music movement.

Source: Typescript, Hanns Eisler Archives.
In EGW III/1, pp. 198–203 the German text was incorporated into the more extensive French version. It bears the title, *Über die DAMB in Deutschland/Les expériences du mouvement musical ouvrier en Allemagne* (DAMB–German Workers' Music Movement). It was read at a music conference in Paris in December 1933, though it must have been written, at least in part, before fascism took power.

1 The "Egmont" overture is a well-known composition by Ludwig van Beethoven and part of the incidental music to the play of the same name by Goethe.

Address to
a Solidarity Concert
1935

Ladies, Gentlemen and Friends,

It is a great honor for me to speak on behalf of my German friends who are now showing such great heroism. So long as we do not read about the underground activities of our friends in Germany it is not so bad, but when we do read about them it is invariably in connection with their being called before a Nazi judge, or being sent to a concentration camp. In recent years we have witnessed crimes against the working class and the intelligentsia in many countries, but the greatest crimes of all have been committed by Hitler. People are quick to forget and therefore it is my duty to remind them of what has occurred. Conditions in Germany should be a lesson to us. The workers and intellectuals of all countries can now see that they alone can help themselves, but if they want to help themselves, they must first arrive at an understanding of their own position. They must rid themselves of their illusions and not say, "It'll get better some day." They must do something to make it better, and that cannot be done without a struggle. In aiding the German working class we also aid ourselves. When we say, "We are internationalists," this is not merely a phrase, an abstract idea or something said out of kindheartedness. Every defeat of the working class in a foreign country weakens the American working class, and every victory, as in the Soviet Union, contributes to the success of the American workers. The workers and intellectuals of the world are inseparably joined in victory and defeat. If you stop a worker, an intellectual or a student in the streets of London, Paris or Zurich and ask him which men he admires and respects, he will answer Thälmann, the German, Dimitrov, the Bulgarian, Rakosi, the Hungarian, Wissel, the Austrian engineer who was hanged, Münichreiter, who was also hanged, the coal miners of the Asturias in Spain, Tom Mooney and the poor Scottsboro boys and their mothers in America and many more. Although we do not know them personally they are all our friends nonetheless, for we know that their cause is our cause.

I would like to say a few words about the working-class music movement in Germany which Hitler has attempted to destroy. In Germany we felt the effects of the crisis in music in capitalist society very early. The separation between serious and light music grew wider and wider throughout the world. The number of listeners to serious music—classical or modern—grew smaller and smaller, while the growth of cheap music became a danger leading to musical barbarism. It must be realized, too, that the development of the radio and gramophone has spread music on an unprecedented scale all over the world. It is a typical picture of a crisis; the technical possibilities grow, but the cultural level deteriorates. The purpose of music in society is growing more and more questionable and the rift between music and social life is widening. During the last fifteen years modern composers have felt this crisis very deeply; their concerts are less frequented, they have become isolated and have moved farther away from the masses of the people. They have made innumerable experiments in order to find a way out, yet at the end of these fifteen years of experimenting no one knows what modern music should be, or what the right solutions are to its problems.

All these experiments were abstract, the composers tried to fathom what modern music should signify, but did not learn to understand reality and out of reality build their music. At a time of gigantic struggles between the classes, the masters of composition gaped at the skies and haggled like fishwives over their wares, as to whose fish smelt better and whose music was more modern. I do not wish to appear prejudiced. These experiments have resulted in some practical good and have prepared material for new music, but the question facing modern music is, who writes it for whom? Today, when we have gathered so much material, a composer can no longer say that he is experimenting. Of the modern musicians I consider Arnold Schönberg to be the greatest, and this genius also had to leave Germany because he is a Jew. What I have mentioned here were typical problems of musical life in Germany before Hitlerism.

Is there a way out? We think the only way out is in an alliance of the working class and progressive intellectuals. The working class must educate the intellectuals to think and act politically, while the intellectuals must bring musical knowledge to the working class. This was furiously opposed by the fascists, who called the progressive intellectuals cultural Bolshevists. Much has been written in the press about the great bourgeois artists who have been exiled. But we must not forget that the lot of the organizers of the workers' music societies is much more tragic. They have suffered a much worse fate. Many of them are imprisoned, most of them have lost their livelihood. More tragic, after all, than that a famous conductor can now only earn dollars and pounds, is the fact that a whole generation of modern young composers, who had joined hands with the working class, have been silenced and have had their artistic development halted. That is a much greater danger for music in Germany than for a virtuoso to be absent. In the two years of the fascist regime, Hitler has succeeded in lowering the standards of music in Germany enormously. Also in the field of music Germany is threatened with barbarism.

Why did Hitler consider this music movement so dangerous that he had to destroy it? Bourgeois music insists that its only function is music. This is the same as if an architect were to say that he builds houses for the sake of building houses, but not so that people can live in them.

This apparent aimlessness of bourgeois music has in reality the very important function of supporting capitalism. People are diverted from their troubles. The hungry, it is true, are not fed, but they are consoled by music and to the cold is vouchsafed a glimpse of a higher world. Proletarian music, on the other hand, is not aimless, but wants to aid and further the struggle for freedom of the workers and intellectuals. This will also be of help to music. Even if the beginnings of proletarian music are very often primitive, because the working class is poor and has to struggle to acquire a musical education, yet it learns from the decay of capitalist music that the working class and the intellectuals are the only sections of the people who will be able to take over the great heritage of bourgeois music and build a new music culture. This is a difficult task, but no matter how great the obstacles it is a problem we have to solve. Our militant art was forbidden by Hitler and all its supporters were rigorously persecuted, so that Hitler could rid himself of a dangerous enemy. But revolutionary music in Germany cannot be forbidden. Traditional revolutionary music, the forbidden songs go illegally from mouth to mouth. They are a distinctive feature and one day will be the signal for the general attack by the workers and middle-class intellectuals on Hitler's bloody dictatorship.

In closing, allow me to make a few remarks about this evening's program. A revolutionary composer has three tasks. The first is agitational and propagandistic, the second is technical experiment in orchestral works and film music, and the third is pedagogic–finding new methods necessary for the musical education of the working class. Today, unfortunately, we can only demonstrate some of our agitation and propaganda work. However, this should not allow us to forget the other tasks.

Finally, I wish to thank all those who helped arrange this evening for the benefit of the children of Hitler's victims; and to thank my friends the singers, whose fine spirit of solidarity made this possible.

Friends and comrades, in memory of our heroic fighters in Germany, let us close our ranks and carry the fight forward with greater intensity. It cannot be said too often that fascism in any and every form means barbarism, mass distress, chaos and war. Everyone, whether he be worker, professor or white collar worker must fight fascism as his main enemy. An important weapon in this fight is solidarity with all victims of fascism!

Long live the international solidarity of all anti-fascists!

Source: Typescript, in English, Hanns Eisler Archives.
EGW III/1, pp. 266-69.
This article covers Eisler's speeches during a tour of the United States in spring 1935 on behalf of anti-fascist solidarity. The English translation by Elie Siegmeister, published in Eisler's Collected Works has been edited for this book.

Letter to Ernst Hermann Meyer in London

On the way to San Francisco

March 14, 1935

Dear Ernst,

Please excuse me for not having written before, and also explain it to all our friends. I am very harassed and it is no great fun, after all the work in London and without a holiday. My meetings are very interesting. The biggest one was in New York with 4,500 people in the audience, a record number that surprised me. There is the greatest poverty in this country that is possible to imagine. Quantitatively, I have never before seen such hunger, squalor and crime against the poor. Chicago, for example, is hell on an unprecedented scale. Traveling from place to place is most instructive. Here is where dictatorship is practised without a "superstructure," and where generations go to wrack and ruin. Our movement here has a mighty resilience. It is young, fresh and with a colossal militancy. I have been to Pittsburgh, a hell of all hells. I take my hat off to these people who go into the struggle and prove themselves in struggle so hard and brutal it beggars description. Unless you have seen America you only know capitalism in part. Here is its most naked, most savage and most brutal form. That is indeed instructive for someone who is inclined to theorize. My very heartiest greetings to all,

Your old Hanns

Source: Original in the possession of Professor Ernst Hermann Meyer, composer and musicologist, Berlin.
EGW III/6 (in preparation).

On Schönberg
1935

Concerning Arnold Schönberg[1] and his place in modern music, Eisler made the following statement:

"Schönberg is my teacher. I am immensely thankful to him for what he has done for me. I consider him the greatest modern bourgeois composer. If the bourgeoisie do not like his music that is regrettable for they have no better composer. To the uninitiated listener Schönberg's music does not sound beautiful because it mirrors the capitalist world as it is without embellishment and because out of his work the face of capitalism stares directly at us. Due to his genius and complete mastery of technique, this face, revealed so starkly, frightens many. Schönberg, however, has performed a tremendous historical service. When his music is heard in the concert halls of the bourgeoisie they are no longer charming and agreeable centers of pleasure where one is moved by one's own beauty but places where one is forced to think about the chaos and ugliness of the world or else turn one's face away.

"As the teacher of generations of young composers Schönberg has performed another great service. For some time to come one will be able to learn from his works, even when they are no longer listened to for enjoyment. In another domain, Einstein's theories although of no practical use in the immediate present are historically of great significance. So with Schönberg. For the past forty years Schönberg's versatility has been of such significance that we, who do not share but reject his political opinions, can admire him as an artist. As Marx put it: "No matter what he thinks about his own situation, or what his views are—

the important thing is to study his actual work, that which he has concretely done." Therefore we can say that Schön-berg's production is, historically, the most valuable of all modern music. Young composers, and above all young proletarian composers, must not listen to or copy him uncritically, they must have the strength to differentiate the content of his work from the method.

"That this man, at sixty years of age and no longer in good health, should be driven homeless throughout the world after a life of severe privations undergone for the sake of his art, is one of the shames of capitalism in the sphere of culture today.

"When today's fashionable composers have long been forgotten, one will still be able to learn from him."

Source: *New Masses,* New York, Feb. 26, 1935.
EGW III/1, pp. 272-73.
This translation, slightly edited for this book, was in the form of an interview titled, "Eisler, Maker of Red Songs" by Ashley Pettis.

1   Arnold Schönberg (1874–1951), emigrated from Ger-many to the U.S.A. in 1933. Taught in Boston and New York; in 1934 took up a teaching post at University of Southern California in Los Angeles. Schönberg's situation at that time was most precarious. In reviewing the year 1934 he wrote, "I cannot deny that there have been more disappointments, troubles and illnesses than I have ever experienced before."

The Birth
of a Worker's Song
1935

Papenburg is a concentration camp in East Friesland, a part of Northern Germany. Here 5,000 German workers were kept prisoner. The surroundings of the concentration camp are foreboding, all around only bog and wasteland. The prisoners were put to working in the swamps digging ditches for drainage. They had to march for two hours to their place of work and two hours back again to the barracks. The work was hard in the extreme. The prisoners had to stand in water up to their knees all day long, digging the ditches with heavy shovels, one of the heaviest of manual labors. With no rubber boots or any gloves, disease spread rapidly among them—rheumatism, gout, heart trouble, eczema and abscesses. The guards treated the prisoners with great severity; the food was unspeakable. To make them still more wretched, they were forbidden to smoke. Only on two afternoons a week, on Wednesdays and Sundays, was smoking allowed. The march to and from work was indescribable. Especially the march back, carrying the heavy implements. Many prisoners collapsed on the way, but were driven on by the guards with blows from their rifle butts.

That was what the camp was like for 5,000 proletarians, Communists, socialists, non-party people and a few intellectuals. Yet they wrote a wonderful song for themselves. The song that was born there is called "The Peatbog Soldiers."[1] The text had to be written in such a way that it could be sung in front of the guards, that is, it had to be camouflaged. This song did not arise spontaneously, as bourgeois folk song experts have assumed. A nucleus among the

77

prisoners set about writing this song in an organized way. What was the main purpose of the song? Why did 5,000 proletarians take the trouble to produce this song, although they had not been able to study poetry or music? Why did they feel urged to do it and how were they able to create such an extraordinary song? We revolutionary professional musicians take off our hats to them in admiration and respect. I consider this song one of the most beautiful revolutionary songs of the international working-class movement. It does not surprise us revolutionaries to see what a tremendous impact can be made by groups of class-conscious workers on the cultural front.

The purpose of this song was to raise the morale of those comrades who were not so politically stable, to give them courage and to create a community spirit on the march. During the first months in the camp the prisoners had to sing the songs suggested by the SA, patriotic songs, soldiers' songs and so on. But the jolly marching tunes of these songs were in crass contrast to the dire state of mind of the prisoners, particularly the politically unstable. The first stage before writing the song was to try and find new words to fit the old soldiers' tunes. This proved inadequate and so a number of draft texts were written by various groups among the politically mature comrades. The best of these drafts was the one chosen for this song. Anyone reading this text without knowing the purpose of it and the way it came to be written may wonder what is revolutionary about it. Yet when you hear it you are overwhelmed to realize how well our imprisoned comrades understood the problem of camouflaging a revolutionary song. The first verses only describe the melancholy hopelessness of their condition. But the last verse!

> But for us there's no complaining
> Winter will in time be past.
> One day we shall cry rejoicing,
> Homeland dear, you're mine at last.

Then we'll march as peatbog soldiers
No more with our spades
To the moor.

The prisoners laid a special emphasis on the words "no more," and note the phrase, "Homeland dear, you're mine at last." This text cannot be separated from its truly wonderful melody, which continues the tradition of the old songs of the sixteenth and seventeenth centuries in Germany. The question arises as to how the modern industrial proletariat knew the songs of the Middle Ages so well that they could lean on this style without having had special musical tuition. The answer is that in the working-class youth movement they liked singing songs from the revolutionary peasant uprisings of the sixteenth century and from the Thirty Years' War, directed against the invasion of the predatory Swedes. The first four bars of the melody of the "Peatbog Soldiers" are a note for note quotation from a song of the Thirty Years' War, with the following words.

Children, listen to the wind howling
Howling against the windows.
Children, where Tilly wreaks havoc
Specters are dwelling.

Tilly was the famous general of the Thirty Years' War. The next passage of the song is a new type development of this quotation. The refrain is actually a more modern formulation, reminiscent of certain military songs, also in conformity with the content of the song, "The Peatbog Soldiers." The peculiar construction of the refrain in major, with the verse in minor, is reminiscent of the Russian revolutionary Funeral March. There too the refrain is in major. Summarizing one can say that the musical form of the song is a sort of montage of various elements, though a song put together in such a way does not prevent it from being new in itself and having a new sort of effect.

Sung to this melody the text has a mournful character, but rises to a wild climax. The remarkable thing is that despite the grief, an optimistic feeling always comes out in the refrain, intensifying towards the end especially with the words, "No more with our spades."

The comrades who brought me this song said that this verse was always sung with particular fervor and was the reason for the appeal of the whole song. Our comrades reported that the SA and the police guards were absolutely amazed that suddenly a new song was being sung on the march by the prisoners. They had learnt it in the barracks of Camp I–there were five camps in Papenburg–and so it was sung freshly and vigorously by a large group of prisoners. The rumor that a new song had been written spread like wildfire through the working detachments and the other camps. Every prisoner wanted to learn it and so an active smuggling went on from camp to camp. The amazement of the guards was indeed great, yet even with a magnifying glass they were not able to discover anything Communist or socialist in the text. In addition it sounded splendid and so the guards were also enthusiastic. Many SA and SS men asked for copies of the song so that they could take it home to learn. I have been told that the song also had an extraordinary effect on the SA guards and is connected with the following incident. When the SA camp guards were dissolved and replaced by a reliable police force, some of the SA men proposed to the prisoners that the whole camp should flee together over the adjacent Dutch border. Thinking it a provocation, the prisoners turned the proposal down. But during their last night's watch some SA men entered the barracks secretly, woke the prisoners and with tears in their eyes begged forgiveness for what they had done to them.

Of course, this is not due to the song alone. But it, too, had helped in influencing the SA. But most of all it helped the mishandled, exhausted and starving comrades on the march and gave the people and the guards a picture of defiance, strength and unbroken will. When a group of prisoners sang the song it was an event for the people of the countryside and for this reason "The Peatbog Soldiers" was forbidden by the district military commander, despite the fact that no political implications could be found in it.

But this song cannot be forbidden, the German workers outside the camps already know it. Many workers of other countries know it and in the next few years it will encircle the world. It is a revolutionary document of great significance and one of the most marvelous revolutionary songs created by the revolutionary working class.

Source: *Bericht über die Entstehung eines Arbeiterliedes,* Typescript, Hanns Eisler Archives.
EGW III/1, pp. 274-78.
Article written in 1935 in New York during Eisler's solidarity tour, probably for publicity work of organizing committee. A stenciled copy of the shortened English version was among Eisler's posthumous papers.

1   According to the singer Mordecai Baumann the "Peatbog Soldiers' Song" climaxed the musical part of every meeting, and became known throughout the country. The song was written by prisoners in the concentration camp Börgermoor near Papenburg, in Northern Germany in August 1933. The words were written by a miner named Esser, and the actor Wolfgang Langhoff, who later became General Director of the Deutsche Theater, Berlin. The four part male chorus was composed by Rudi Goguel, a white–collar worker. A chorus of sixteen sang it for the first time at a performance called the "Circus Conzentrani." The song became known publicly through released prisoners. Eisler heard of it in January 1935 in London, through someone who later turned out to be an informer of the Gestapo. Eisler made an arrangement to the melody and provided a piano accompaniment.

A Musical Journey
through America
1935

Ladies and Gentlemen,
The journey that I am going to tell you about took me
from London to New York and from New York across the
whole of America to the Pacific Coast. Impressions of a
journey should not only be enjoyable to the listener, they
should also be useful. To this I must say: seeing distant
lands and getting to know other social relations, habits
and customs give us an opportunity to test our methods of
reasoning. When we think that we have found the right
method of reasoning, that is, the right point of view concerning the behavior of people one to another, to social
problems, to art and problems of art, then these methods
should be applicable not only in our own country, but they
should be valid, under other conditions, and for other
people, for today there are far more ties between peoples
than we are aware of.

What are the differences between peoples? Aren't there
rich and poor all over the world, exploiter and exploited?
Aren't classes struggling against each other everywhere?
Certainly the nuances of these struggles are different. But
only the forms are different–different only in at what stage
they occur but not in content. The world is in an appalling
crisis and people everywhere are seeking a class solution to
this crisis. This is particularly true of America, which is in
the center of the crisis. The United States feels this partic-
ulary because the American worker was among the most
highly paid in the world between 1918 and 1927, and American business made the highest profits.

If, Ladies and Gentlemen, you find it strange for a

modern composer to begin the account of his travels with economic questions, then do bear in mind that music in particular and above all modern music has reacted most violently to this crisis. Today music and society can no longer be regarded as naively as the artists regarded it thirty years ago, and as mediocre imitators regard it even today. Modern American composers in particular have learnt in these hard years that music is not ethereal, unaffected by reality, but that music like every art mirrors the life of society and the class struggle. That is not at all strange. Since music is man-made, it is subordinated to the general laws of mankind and consequently of human society. In America, especially, it is interesting to observe that the best composers think along these lines and that these ideas can be found in their works.

Now let me tell you about the stages of my journey.

First, there was the sea voyage from London to New York. You have certainly often heard and read about modern ships, the big turbine steamships of 47,000 tons, so that further technicalities are superfluous. But one thing is interesting about a journey of this kind. Three hundred years ago it was a great personal accomplishment for a ship's captain and his crew to hazard such a voyage. The risk was great, and only succeeded because of the captain, his personality, his ability, his courage, his presence of mind and the iron discipline which he demanded of his crew. The literature of all peoples glorifies the bold heroes of the sea, discovering new lands at the risk of their own lives and those of their crews. Today these heroes of the sea have vanished and for a simple reason. They are no longer required. Technology has made a voyage from London to New York or from London to India just as simple as an express train journey from Paris to Prague. The hero of the sea has become the official of the sea. On board ship it is so organized that the risk is practically nil. Only the bad conditions for the sailors and the service personnel remain. No longer heroes and personalities, but officials wield the iron discipline. The purpose of seafaring is no longer romantic, but is a profit-making undertaking of a joint stock company. For instance, a ship crossing regularly between London and New York has at any given hour of the voyage the same course and the same geographical position. Radio service provides such exact weather reports that the presence of mind of the captain has become superfluous. Like the steering of the ship, everything else is mechanized. Though the sailor does not sing shanties any more, nor brave the storms his work is extremely arduous and monotonous, mostly cleaning the ship, painting the hull and assisting in the landing. Not a glimmer of romance surrounds him either, he is a worker, a proletarian.

Why are such observations necessary? It is necessary and useful because this process of technology which makes the hero, the captain, superfluous in modern society is not only to be found at sea, but can also be found in any big factory. One hundred years ago a private employer had to have a forceful personality, but even he was made superfluous through modern methods of production. So on a sea voyage we can see that the development of the material forces of production in society has led to the changing of man himself. Personalities in the old sense no longer exist, but a new type of personality, of hero, who does not advance at the detriment of the majority of society, but who rises with his class by fighting for the interests of his class, is coming into being.

You have often heard, I am sure, of New York City's fantastic skyline. As our ship approached the harbor at eight o'clock in the morning I too was impressed with its grandeur. But how different were my thoughts from those who had arrived in New York fifteen years ago during the time of prosperity and boom. I looked at the skyscrapers and asked myself apprehensively who lives in them, they must be empty. For I knew that in America 20 million people were in need of public assistance, that is 20 million unemployed and short-time workers! When I saw the giant

Brooklyn Bridge, this triumph of technology, I asked myself uneasily if the people who had to cross it daily had empty stomachs.

A walk through 42nd Street in New York is something extraordinary. Just imagine that there is not simply one Strasbourg Cathedral, but two hundred of them, all built one next to the other, so that giant towers enclose the narrow streets, then you will know what a daily walk in downtown New York is like.

The elevator operators are enormously important for such a building is useless without a whole series of elevators. On the fourth day of my visit the elevator operators threatened to strike. Their conditions were miserable and the employers refused to meet their demands. Their work is difficult and nerve-racking. Just imagine what it is like to go up and down eighty stories for eight hours daily. A strike among them would mean that it would not be possible to deliver the mail and since the buildings house mostly business firms no clients or other agents would come. And there, I asked myself, what is the good of these big skyscrapers, designed by brilliant architects, if the elevator boys aren't willing to work under any conditions. Now who does the skyscraper belong to and who gives it its value, if without the elevator operators it becomes a pile of old metal. America, with its enormous technical development, gives us food for thought along such lines every day.

The Metropolitan Opera House is in New York as you know. It is one of the most famous opera houses in the world. I was indeed looking forward to visiting it. But I had only been in New York for a week when all the papers carried the news of a crisis in the Metropolitan Opera, saying that if a large sum running into millions of dollars was not found immediately, it might have to close. So I made inquiries as to who owns the opera house and whom it benefits. I heard the following: It belongs to a private company of millionaires and represents a kind of private luxury for the wealthiest people of New York. New

York City, together with its suburbs has over ten million inhabitants, of which, at the most, 30,000 to 50,000 are able to go to the opera. But the wealthy no longer feel inclined to maintain this institution. Since ordinary mortals are not interested in opera, its closure is imminent. On my return journey I read in the papers that a few millionaires had written out some checks, so that next year the opera will still be able to keep going. But there were also voices among the workers, employees and intellectuals demanding that this opera house be taken away from the wealthy and turned into a publicly supported institution for the masses of the people by means of a special tax. The wealthy were incensed and said it was a political question, and altogether degrading to draw such a noble institution into such a low debate.

New York concert life is prodigiously big and diverse. The best virtuosi, composers and conductors are engaged, so that the programs are absolutely crammed with famous names. However, the admission to these concerts is very high and they are attended by a diminishing number of people thus becoming a privilege of the wealthy. Ordinary folk have to listen to music by radio broadcasts or at popular concerts, if they cannot satisfy their musical needs in one of the countless cinemas.

However, some groups of modern musicians occupy a special position in New York concert life. One of these groups is a section of the International Music Society, also well-known over here. As you know this is an association of modern composers who give a series of annual concerts. Sad to say, this association has a very small circle of supporters. I attended a concert where the well-known Pro Arte String Quartet from Brussels gave the first performance of a quartet by Bartók, the famous Hungarian composer, among other pieces. One might have expected that the first performance of a work by an internationally renowned modern composer performed by one of the best string quartets in the world would have aroused a certain amount of interest. Unfortunately, the concert was held in a small hall and moreover it was only half filled. No more than 200 people were present. An American friend told me that this is always the case. These unfortunate facts only prove that modern music is isolated from the masses to a great extent, and is no part of the realities of social life. This has already been acknowledged by a number of the best American composers. They were of the opinion that it is not only the fault of the public, but also the fault of modern music. Modern composers live, as you might say, in an ivory tower, cut off from reality. Their works do not reflect the great struggles of man against man. Their works express only their inner emotions or are of a purely technical character, of interest only to experts. Modern music which we all love and for which we are prepared to fight must finally come out of its isolation and conquer the ear of the masses, the workers, employees and intellectuals. This can only be done, however, if music considers the interests of these people and understands the necessity of taking part in the struggles being waged by them for their existence and for the construction of a new, better order of society. Modern music should no longer be mere distraction for the idle wealthy; it must turn to the masses of the people and support their just struggle. For us Europeans these ideas are not new. Many composers have been fighting for them for some years. Yet I was impressed on finding these ideas so fresh, so strong and courageous among the best composers of America. This group of modern composers has set up an organization, called the New York Composers' Collective. A number of the best talents belong to it and among them are: Copland, Riegger, Cowell, Seeger and Siegmeister. These are but a few of the composers who are active in this Collective. Sympathetic to it, however, are a number of internationally renowned experts, for example, the composer Roger Sessions, the conductor Leopold Stokowski and the Boston conductor Nicolas Slonimsky, particularly well-known for his interpretation of modern works. This Collective is perhaps one of the most interesting associations of modern composers in existence today. Every year they publish a collection of vocal works for the working class. Excellent songs and choral pieces in great number can be found in these collections. I would like to make myself quite clear. These composers are struggling against antiquated, sterile music, against the kitschy kind of film and jazz music, and against snobbish, isolated modern concert music. They are struggling for a new modern style based upon the latest achievements of modern music, while using it at the same time in the struggle of the workers and employees against oppression and for bread and freedom. This Composers' Collective gives a series of concerts which are well attended by all strata of the New York population.

After New York the next city I visited was Pittsburgh. It is the center of the coal and steel industry in America. I must say, if you want to describe hell on earth, then you only have to describe Pittsburgh. It is a fearful hell of cold, hunger and degradation of man by man. The city of Pittsburgh consist of 5 percent elegant business and residential areas and 95 percent misery.

The music life is restricted to an even smaller circle of the wealthy than in New York. The Pittsburgh Symphony Orchestra gives a number of concerts annually under the baton of very famous conductors. On the other hand, cultural life for the masses is meager in the extreme. With over a million inhabitants, Pittsburgh has no permanent theater and no popular concerts. The only entertainment and distraction for the working people is the movies. All the same, the example of the New York modern music movement is being copied in Pittsburgh. The Pittsburgh workers are setting up their first cultural organizations, their first music associations; they are fighting not only for a better life, but together with the music intellectuals for culture as well.

From Pittsburgh we went on to Chicago. Chicago has

four and a half million inhabitants. It is a very interesting city, wonderfully situated on Lake Michigan. Along the lake front the gigantic skyscrapers and business districts lie next to the homes of the wealthy. Behind them sprawls the actual city of Chicago. The residential areas around the big slaughterhouses are fearful to see. The stockyards and slaughterhouses one next to the other and the meat packing factories are crisscrossed by a colossal network of railway tracks. After visiting the stockyards, some people cannot eat meat for a time, due to sentimentality or weak nerves. I have no patience with people who pale when cattle are slaughtered, but who didn't seem to mind when people were slaughtering each other in the last World War, and who now want to start a new war. Yet it's not only in war that people slaughter each other, they do it every day. Every day people die of hunger and disease. Frightful injustices are daily occurrences; exploitation and the arrogance of parasites daily take their toll of the working people. This is when we should have nervous attacks and turn pale. This is when we should get sentimental. And it is also when we should learn to combat the slaughter of man by man.

These were my thoughts after visiting Chicago's stockyards, for they seemed symbolic of our society.

My journey continued via Denver, Buffalo Bill's town, not only because there is a memorial to him in the mountains, but because there is a still bigger one in the hearts of all little boys who love Red Indian stories. From Denver onwards the immense range of the Rocky Mountains begins. The city of the Mormons, a religious sect, was founded on the banks of the enormous Salt Lake in the mountains: Salt Lake City, Utah. Today these religious fanatics have become modern businessmen.

For a whole day the railroad runs through the highlands until it sinks in the western part of the range and a friendly blue sky announces that we are in the West. Seventy years ago the West had something fabulous about it. There was gold, precious metals and oil; there was magnificent vegetation. "Go West Young Man" was the slogan of a whole generation between 1848 and 1880. When you come down from the snow-capped Sierra Nevada you believe you are in a garden: orange groves, a profusion of flowers and houses light and airy.

San Francisco is one of the most beautiful cities in the world. The music life there derives its distinctive character through the composer Henry Cowell, who lives and works there. Cowell heads the group of International Modern Music and is a lecturer in musicology at the university. He is well-known in Europe as a composer. His specialty is collecting the folk music of the Cubans, Mexicans and Indians; he has one of the largest existing collections of gramophone records of this genre. He has also issued gramophone records of Indian music himself. He is a distinguished musicologist, whose papers on music are published in the best music periodicals.

From San Francisco I flew to Hollywood. This much celebrated Hollywood is actually only a suburb of Los Angeles, the center of the rich Californian oil wells. Hollywood itself looks like a piece of film scenery that has not yet been dismantled. The reason for such light structures are the annual earthquakes which damage a considerable number of houses. Hollywood and Los Angeles are proper movie towns. Practically every inhabitant has something to do with films. But there is a marked difference between the fabulous fees paid to the stars and those paid to that large group of small actors, extras and film maintenance workers. At present 22,000 unemployed actors are going hungry in Los Angeles. They are faced with poverty, while a film star in vogue at the moment earns up to 500,000 dollars a year, that is about 17 million French francs.

My visit to Metro-Goldwyn-Mayer, a big film company, was of great interest. I have worked in many film studios—in Paris and in London—but we have nothing in Europe to compare with the perfect organization and technical equipment. As a composer I was chiefly interested in the music studios. To my great astonishment I found new microphones, which we do not yet know about. They are no longer shaped like cylinders, but are spherical. The offices of the composers and music arrangers are very strange. When a cinema audience looks at a Hollywood film it may well believe that the music has been written by one more or less talented composer. In reality it is quite different. The music is written by a number of people and on the following principle. The company has five or six composers and arrangers sitting in offices. They are not excessively well paid and are in fact music office workers, for they have to keep to appointed office hours every day, even if they have nothing to do. The composers are selected according to their special genres. One is chosen as a specialist in military music, (he was previously an army musician in Germany). Another is for Vienna waltzes and operetta music of the old school. Yet another is a specialist for jazz and dance music, still another for lyrics and the last writes the preludes and the accompaniments–he comes from serious music. Now if a director has a film ready and needs a jazz number, then it's the turn of number three. If he wants a military march, it's number one's turn. If he requires some symphonic accompaniment music in a particular part of the film, then it is the turn of the one with classical training. That is how the music to a film is composed, with five or six composers. From the point of view of rationalization, the film industry is not so foolish, but what hell for the composers, who year after year have to write the same type of music and thus are faced with the prospect of becoming hopelessly dim-witted. In addition, the standard of most of these films is abominably low, not only in subject matter, but also in music. Although films could be an excellent means of entertainment and education in modern society, in the hands of private industry they are solely for profit and a means of lulling the masses.

From Los Angeles I went to St. Louis and from there to Detroit, the center of the world motorcar industry, with a population of about 900,000. Detroit is a relatively young city. Almost every worker in Detroit at some time or other has worked for Ford. For years Henry Ford's motorcar company was capitalism's greatest achievement. It was even said that Ford had found the way to save capitalism, and that in his factory the workers were so well off they didn't need to fight for their rights and for political power. But the crisis has also destroyed this delusion. The Ford workers are in a bad way. Ford has a work force of 70,000. However, the work is so planned that on an average every Ford worker only works four to five months a year. His daily wage is from 3 to 4 dollars, so that after deductions he has about 100 dollars a month. But since a Ford worker only works for four to five months, the money he earns has to last for the whole year. The working methods at Ford's are inhuman. Our writers and composers should be sent there to see this hell and tell the world what our times mean for some people in degradation, hopelessness and brutality. Suffice to say, if you stand at the main gate to one of the big plants at the end of a shift, you will see the workers jam themselves into the streetcars. Two minutes later they fall into an exhausted sleep, a twofold exhaustion, physical and mental. The terrible monotony of the work can be compared to opening and shutting a matchbox eight to ten hours a day nonstop for ten years. And this without any hope that this senseless occupation will feed or clothe you and your family anywhere adequately, or to educate your children for a better future. The car market is saturated. There are too many cars and too few buyers, so that this speedup is in glaring contradiction to the market conditions. But such speedup lowers the cost of production and that is why it is brutally enforced.

From Detroit I returned to New York. My journey had been indeed interesting and instructive, for I had had the opportunity of studying how music related to society in a country new to me. In New York the following news awaited me. The Secretariat of the First International Workers' Music Olympiad had invited me to Strasbourg to take over the chairmanship of the jury and to deliver a lecture. I accepted this invitation with great pleasure for I believe that this Music Olympiad can be of great significance for modern music. It begins on June 8th with an international concert in the Orangery. I am glad to be able to inform you that a number of internationally famous composers will be taking part. Among them are my friend the composer Alan Bush, Professor at the Royal Academy of Music in London, the noted writer on music Dr. Reichmann from Czechoslovakia and Fritz Hugo from Switzerland.

The best names in European modern music are on the honorary committee of this Olympiad. Alongside writers such as Romain Rolland and Henri Barbusse are also the most important French composers, Darius Milhaud and Arthur Honegger.

Ladies and Gentlemen, you might wonder why the best composers in Europe and the most famous writers view with such sympathy and attention the Strasbourg International Workers' Music Olympiad. In the foregoing I have tried to clarify for you the peculiar situation in modern music, which, as you know, is calamitous. Despite the growth of the means of production in music, such as radio, sound film and records, the standards in music are deteriorating. The best composers maintain that we are living at a time of musical barbarism and illiteracy. Those who understand the great traditions of classical music are diminishing, while the stultifying influence of cheap music is growing. Just as everyone is looking for a way out in the economic crisis, so we modern composers are looking for ways and means of overcoming the crisis in music. We can only overcome it if we have a mass basis. There is a whole new group of people who are fighting not only for their economic rights, but also for a new culture. We music experts must form an alliance with them: they are the workers, the working proletariat. The First International Workers' Music Olympiad offers us the practical possibility of forming such an alliance, and for this reason it is of tremendous importance. We artists should at long last realize the moral aspects of our profession. The Workers' Music Olympiad is taking place as a part of the struggle against fascism, against war. We artists would not be worthy of the great heritage of classical music and our great masters, Bach, Beethoven and Mozart, were we not to fight on the side of the working class. For they alone represent the cause of justice, of truth and of culture, and thus also the cause of modern music as opposed to falsehood, oppression and cultural barbarism. Because the best brains in music have declared themselves for the workers on the occasion of the First International Workers' Music Olympiad we hope that after the Olympiad is over this alliance will mean the beginning of a new international music movement.

Source: *Musikalische Reise durch Amerika,* Typescript, Hanns Eisler Archives.
EGW III/1, pp. 282-95.
Eisler read this report of his American tour in the Strasbourg broadcasting station on June 7, 1935, during the First International Workers' Music Olympiad. Transmission was broken off, however, when Eisler described the brutal working conditions in the Ford Motor Company.

Problems
of Working-Class Music
Interview with Hanns Eisler
1935

Mr. Eisler, what place does the working-class music move-
ment occupy at this time when great events and changes are
taking place, and where people and ideas are being re-
evaluated?

The working-class music movement indeed plays a great
part in the cultural life of the proletariat, but we must
admit that it is not at the level of the working-class movement in general. Many working-class music organizations
and choral societies perform music which is antiquated
and out of step with the political struggle today or is even
in contradiction to it. So we often find that there are
wonderful organizations whose activities do not reflect the
class consciousness of the progressive sections of the working people.

Is there already considerable new revolutionary music?

There is more than is generally known. The fact that little
of it is known is due to sabotage by the bourgeois music
industry. It is our job to popularize modern revolutionary
music so that the forces lagging behind can catch up with
the avant-garde.

Wouldn't it be useful for the associations if you were to
mention some of the representatives of modern revolution-
ary music?

In America there is Jacob Schaeffer, perhaps one of the
most important composers. He was a carpenter, who devel-

oped into a composer and conductor. His is an extraordinary talent. He has written a great deal of music from simple mass songs to big oratorios. In addition in America there are composers of international repute such as Copland, Riegger, Seeger, Swift, Cowell and many others, who come from modern bourgeois music circles, but who have written a number of extremely valuable and interesting works for the working-class movement. In England there is the very well-known modern composer Alan Bush, Professor at the Royal Academy of Music in London. He conducts a workers' choir. He has written some excellent works for the movement and is generally considered the most important representative of young English music. Darius Milhaud and Honegger in France are sympathizers with our movement. Alois Hába and Erwin Schulhoff are the most important representatives of our movement in Czechoslovakia. For instance, Schulhoff has written a big choral work entitled "Unite!" This choral piece uses extracts from the Communist Manifesto as text. The young composer Mortensen who comes from Denmark, the highly talented Hungarian Ferenc Szábo in Moscow, whose works are enormously popular in the Soviet Union, are also important international representatives of workers' music. Of the Soviet Russian composers Shostakovich should be mentioned first. He is one of the most gifted composers of his age and has aroused great excitement throughout the world. He is still very young and one can expect great things from him. Those are just a few names. I could mention many more of those who are still younger and who should help further the movement. Among the broad masses of the working people the works of these composers are unfortunately not sufficiently known.

Don't technical difficulties also prevent this modern revolutionary music from becoming known?

Yes. There are enormous difficulties for the following reasons. Through the intensive practice of the traditional late romantic nineteenth century music, working-class singers and musicians have acquired a certain musical taste and habit of music-making. This does not help, but hinders the performance of modern works. For instance, a choir that for years has been singing pieces like *Freiheit, wir warten dein* (Freedom, we await thee) or *Die blasse Wasserlilie* (The Pale Waterlily) has become so used to singing homophonic music that they have great difficulties when a change is made to polyphonic music. It is not always the working-class singers or musicians who do not understand modern workers' music, often enough it is the complete lack of understanding on the part of the choir master and conductor that prevents the performances of modern choral works. That too is understandable, but popularizing modern revolutionary working-class music on a mass scale is dependent on the education of these music functionaries. This new music is in every way suited to and useful for the political struggle of the working class.

Undoubtedly the educational development of choir masters and conductors is vitally necessary, but doesn't this also depend on the attitude of the working-class singers and musicians?

That, too, is another of the main questions. A revolutionary working-class singer or musician must first learn to be critical in matters of art, and not just be admiring or worshiping. He must not be taken in by "beauty," but must ask himself, does it help him and his class, or is it useless or even damaging. Just as we demand critical thinking from comrades in political life, so in the same way must we demand critical thinking in art.

You spoke about antiquated music. What do you consider for instance is antiquated in the programs of an average Alsace-Lorraine or Swiss choir or musical association?

If we go through the programs, we find the following music pieces which I think are very bad and antiquated. For example, a number of extraordinarily stupid marches of martial character, or old-fashioned overtures by inferior composers. These are in every way capable of spoiling musical taste. Choral literature is still worse. These abominable texts which say nothing, set to bombastic and hypocritical music! It has always been a nightmare for me to think of eighty choir members appearing on the platform and meltingly singing *Ich warte dein* (I await thee). Then these "nature moods," these false folk songs, in short, kitsch, bad music and false words.

One might conclude from your answer that you are against folk songs!

You cannot say folk songs in general! First, there are two sorts of folk songs, the genuine and the false. The genuine folk song originated in earlier centuries from the people themselves. The false folk song is the product of a corrupt and sordid entertainment industry which "borrows" the idiom of the genuine folk song, only in a coarser and distorted form. We have to combat this false folk song because it is ghastly kitsch. On the other hand, the genuine folk song can be extremely valuable, both from the point of view of text as well as of music, and is genuine folk culture. But here, too, we must be critical. Too little is known among working-class singers about the way bourgeois research workers handed these songs down to them. In the most important collection of folk songs published by Erk[1], which today is still the basis of all songbooks, the publisher informs us in his foreword that he cut out all politically unsuitable and all morally obnoxious songs. This means nothing less than that the most valuable folk songs are unkown to the broad mass of the working class. The bourgeoisie exercised a sort of censorship to expunge everything that they considered offensive. But what does the bourgeoisie consider politically offensive? For instance, the wonderful songs of the Peasant Wars, a really genuine revolutionary folk art; then the robust, original work songs and love songs, these were expunged because they did not conform to the moral attitude of a middling German schoolteacher. So we will also have to decide between the good and the bad in folk songs. Revolutionary folk song researchers will have the job of sorting out the grain from the chaff. Apart from this, among genuine folk songs some are good and some are bad!

Are there any modern folk songs?

If by folk song we mean a song that is sung everywhere, then yes. But if we mean a song that has been made by the people, then on the whole, no. Folk songs arise under primitive economic conditions, especially in agrarian economies. Modern capitalism is unsuitable ground for the growth of folk songs. Folk culture is dying off just as the handicrafts are. But we have something else–the mass song. The mass song is the fighting song of the modern working class and is to a certain degree, folk song at a higher stage than before, because it is international.

Is the fighting song the only form of revolutionary music?

No, we have already developed a great number of forms, mass songs, polyphonic choral pieces, didactic pieces and many more. Now it is the task of the modern revolutionary composers to write special orchestral music for working-class bands. Here the modern composers must take into account the concrete situation and the technical level of each association.

Don't you think that one reason for modern revolutionary music not having the mass basis that we would like it to have lies partly with the composers?

Yes. The modern composer should not cut himself off from the mass movement. It is not enough to sit in his room and write for the working-class movement. He must take an active part in social life and in the struggles of the working class. We must form an alliance between the music intellectuals and the working class. The music intellectual can learn how to think politically and can acquire a revolutionary attitude from the working class. The working class can take over the tradition of great classical music from the music intellectual as well as the methods of new and contemporary music. Only when this alliance has become a fact, will we be able to overcome the difficulties in our movement.

Source: *L'Humanité d'Alsace,* Strasbourg, June 1935, under the headline, *L'Humanité interviewt Hanns Eisler.*
EGW III/8 (in preparation).
The interview was reprinted in *Schweizerische Sänger-Zeitung,* Berne, July 1935, Nos. 13, 14, with the lead-in: "One of our reporters had the opportunity of talking to Hanns Eisler during the Music Olympiad in Strasbourg about some of the burning questions of working-class music. The composer Hanns Eisler, Professor at the New School for Social Research in New York, is famous in the international working-class movement." An editor's note at the end of the article said that while they did not agree with all of Eisler's remarks, "here and there they will set people thinking."

1   Ludwig Christian Erk (1807–1883), greatest 19th century collector of German folk songs, left a collection of over 20,000 song transcripts. The revised edition of his *Deutscher Liederhort,* the most comprehensive collection of German folk songs, was edited in 1893–94 by Franz Magnus Böhme.

Hollywood
Seen from the Left
1935

Hollywood, the film town, the dream of every petty bourgeois, is a sort of suburb of Los Angeles. I flew in bad
weather from San Francisco to Hollywood and at the air-
port exit I found comrades waiting for me. One of them
greeted me with, "Hello, Hanns, how is Schickler Strasse 4
getting on?" I looked at the man and wondered when we
had met and it turned out that he had attended my course
at the Marxist Worker's School. At the time he had been
a reporter for an American paper in Berlin and in the
evenings he went to MASCH. Since this comrade was kind
enough to act as my secretary, I had the opportunity of
really looking at Hollywood from the left.

In the first place Hollywood has the character of a small
provincial town, full of gossip and intrigue. Certainly, this
gossipy town lies bedded in wonderful scenery on the Pacific Ocean, amidst palms and the most glorious flowers.
The film stars live some miles out of Hollywood in Santa
Monica. I talked to many film people, I won't mention
their names, it might harm them because of the reactionary
administration in California. It is no exaggeration to say that
film artists, not only film personnel, but actors, scenarists
and directors are turning to the left, despite the fact that
some are highly paid. (A first-class cameraman earns 1,500
dollars weekly, a good actor between 500 and 1,000 dollars
a week, and a star up to 400,000 dollars a year.) They are
turning to the left because they are disgusted with their
work, because they know it's the end of any art if its only
aim is to make profits for the film industry. One famous
actor got in trouble because they tried to prove that he had

given money to help finance the Communist Party. That nearly cost him his livelihood, and he could only save himself by saying that it was not true and that the whole thing was vicious slander. While I was waiting in the room of the chief story editor of a big film company I asked if I might look at some of the film scripts lying on the table, whereupon he got red in the face and said it wasn't possible. And it is dissatisfaction that is driving the film artists to the left. For a film writer it is unbearable, in the long run, to live in a time of the most important events, full of blood and filth but also full of the heroic struggle of the working class, and, at the same time, to work for a film company which demands that he continually produce the most piffling scripts, completely unrelated to reality, stupidly deceptive, and kitsch. However, the reactionary administration in San Francisco and the film industry maintain a very sharp watch over their employees, even up to the stars, so that these have to camouflage their political sympathies with the working class. All the same there are various ways and means of showing one's sympathy and solidarity in practice.

Charlie Chaplin is still the most popular and most admired actor in America. He is loved by the American people. The most fantastic rumors circulate about his new film.[1] The reactionary Hearst press hastened to open an attack on Chaplin claiming he was making a Communist film. So in order not to be boycotted he had to put out one denial after another in the press and prove that his film is not a Communist one, but a Charlie Chaplin film, though placed in a social setting. He explained in an interview that he is in favor of Communism, because under Communism he will be recognized as the greatest actor in the world. (This is very American, a way of expressing support for Communism.) He has been working on this film for two years and hopes to have it finished in six months. After that Chaplin is planning a film on Schweik[2] by Jaroslav Hašek, with Peter Lorre in the title role.

The music department of a big Hollywood film company is a very peculiar place. Usually, the ordinary movie-goer imagines that the music to a film is written by one composer. In Hollywood it is different. Every factory has five or six music specialists who are permanently employed and who have to keep punctually to their office hours. Number one is a specialist in military music, number two in sentimental love songs, number three is a better trained composer for symphonic music, for overtures and intermezzi, number four is a specialist in Viennese operetta, number five is for jazz. So if music is required for a film, then every composer has to work on a certain section, according to his specialty. The composers have no idea of what is happening in the rest of the film or what his fellow musician is composing, everyone merely does his own particular bit. They say that this is a kind of rationalization of film music, which could be progressive. However, since not only the content of the films, but also the music is usually on a very low level, in a short time these composer-employees are completely stultified through this one-sided type of work. They do not feel very happy about it, but what can they do? Besides that, there is the following method of selecting, let us say, a song. The studio manager, an absolutely unmusical man, will only accept a song that he can sing immediately. Everything else is turned down as being too difficult, although, as I say, he is absolutely unmusical with a voice like a foghorn. But then it is precisely this lack of musical feeling that guarantees that only song hits are acceptable, that is, numbers that you can sing before you have even heard them.

The bit actors and actresses, the so-called extras, are not permanently employed. In Hollywood and Los Angeles there are about 22,000 unemployed extras. Their existence is precarious. They must keep in constant contact with the studios if they do not want to be pushed out of the production process. But you can only remain in contact if you keep your car, for there are no subways in Los Angeles, only a few bus and electric train lines. Indeed, the means of public transportation are purposely kept at a restricted level, because the city council obtains certain concessions from the auto industry magnates. Yet one must remember that Los Angeles and Hollywood together have a million and a half inhabitants. A car alone makes it technically possible to get to the studio straightaway after a telephone call or to make frequent calls on film agents and film companies. In order to keep the car, you have to go hungry.

On the one hand there is insecurity and misery while on the other there is fantastic luxury in Hollywood, as perhaps can be found in no other place in the world: casinos, brothels, luxury hotels and amusement establishments of every imaginable kind. For instance, Palm Springs is a small artificial oasis in the California desert, a few hours distant from Hollywood by car. An incredibly luxurious hotel was built in this desert, complete with gambling club. Every sort of comfort and every conceivable luxury are available at a colossal price. That's how the big film producers and stars spend their weekends; with gambling, drinking, whoring, and one of the most suitable places to do it in without being observed by nosy reporters and blackmailers is Palm Springs.

From time to time the big film companies start moaning about taxation and launch press rumors that they are about to transfer their studios to another country; by that some mean Florida and others New York. That would mean that hundreds of thousands of people whose livelihood is connected with films, would lose their jobs since a journey from Hollywood to New York is over 3,000 miles and is very costly; the film companies, of course, would only take their stars and a small staff with them. The unskilled workers, the extras, the assistant hairdressers, decorators and so on would be taken on locally. When an interesting young film director told me about this I suggested that he make a film out of it with the following story: The film companies transfer to New York, and now the hundreds of thousands permanently thrown out of the production process decide to march the 3,000 miles from Hollywood to New York on foot. A new crusade! For between Hollywood and New York lie vast deserts and the icy peaks of the Rocky Mountains and the dreadful high steppes of the Sierra Nevada. A large number of these people would be bound to perish on the march. But those who would arrive in New York at their masters' door would most likely think differently from when they set out. The film director then said, "That is a marvelous idea for a film, but do you think that the censor will allow it?" I answered, "No!"

Source: Typescript, Hanns Eisler Archives.
EGW III/1, pp. 302–6.
This article was written im June 1935 in Moscow for the German language daily paper *Deutsche Zentralzeitung*.

1   Chaplin's "Communist" film that Eisler mentions, refers to *Modern Times*. It was produced between 1932–36 and was the first of Chaplin's films to deal with contemporary social problems.

2   The idea for the "Schweik" film did not materialize.

Some Remarks on the Situation of the Modern Composer
1935

When medical science was not yet able to diagnose the causes of serious diseases, such as tuberculosis, beri-beri, or diseases of the blood, patients were in a sorry plight. These diseases were considered to be matters of chance, misfortunes for which there was little alleviation, or it was believed the sick were possessed and should be exorcised by prayer. When modern science and technology discovered new methods of diagnosis and new apparatus, it became known that these diseases were not personal disasters, but were caused by microbes and if recognized in time, were curable. Those were the great days of chemotherapy. The latest scientific research has produced a still more interesting result. It has been ascertained that a large number of these diseases, such as tuberculosis and beri-beri, are the result of social conditions, and many of them will disappear entirely when social conditions are changed. What a colossal development of human knowledge—disease, as fate, incurable; disease, caused by bacteria, curable. Disease, caused by social conditions, which are changeable, curable.

If we modern composers were able to apply some of this objectivity, common sense and knowledge to our own field, we would be more successful. But that requires a scientific approach instead of the noncommitted futile natterings about art. This is urgently necessary, since the crisis in modern music is sharpening, while barbarism in music is on the increase.

The people have become musical illiterates, despite technical progress in music. It is high time for contemporary composers to see reason and alter their attitude. In order to contend successfully with this state of anarchy and barbarism a new type of composer, teacher and musician is needed. I would appeal above all, to the modern composer, for as the producers of music, they are the most important. If we wish to create a new type of composer, then we must first challenge the old type wherever we find him. This can only be done with scientific methods, objectively and fairly; therefore it is necessary to raise the practice and theory of music to the level of contemporary thought. Unfortunately, it is true to say that at a time when new methods of working and reasoning have already been introduced in industry, medicine, chemistry, physics, sociology and political economy, wholly antiquated methods are still applied in the theory and practice of music. The so-called modern composer is mainly to blame for this state of affairs. We shall have to find a new definition for the word "modern." After all, it should be possible to determine what, for our time, is progressive or retrogressive in music.

The crisis in music has been caused by the general crisis in society. In music it appears concretely in the technique of composing. This, in turn, has contributed to the complete isolation of modern music from social life. The modern composer has meanwhile become a parasite, supported by wealthy patrons out of personal interests, and no longer carries out any rational work in society. Consequently, the composer's profession still has something of the subservient character of the seventeenth century. He can no longer maintain himself from his compositions, which is already suspect, but for example, has to hang around the salons in order to be seen. That is particularly detrimental to young composers for they are thus cut off from the realities of life. This seclusion leads to most modern works having nothing to say about the most urgent issues of the day. Some modern composers are only concerned with themselves. (So let them!) Others have form and technique problems. (It's a fine thing to contemplate technique, so why disturb them?) Lastly, there are the so-called lyrical temperaments, exquisitely sensitive and profound, who know definitely spring will come and the moon will shine when the nights are light. (That's a boost for Hollywood.) Now modern composers are of the opinion that "absolute music," more accurately music without words, cannot express anything definite at all, and certainly nothing about "the urgent issues of our day." Music without words, they say, cannot achieve this nor is it the purpose of music. (The purpose of music is only to be found in music itself. Music for music's sake.)

But we know from history that so-called absolute music reached the highest point of expression in one particular period. Beethoven's symphonies were the music of the struggle of the young bourgeoisie against decaying feudalism. We also know from history that instrumental music was not always predominant. In the fifteenth and sixteenth centuries instrumental music played a subordinate role to vocal music. Instrumental music and the concert (as the organized form of musical life) are not eternal, but historical forms. They arose and developed within capitalist society and they enter a crisis when capitalist society enters a crisis. In 1750 the Mannheim Symphonic School was new and revolutionary. In 1810 it embodied the highest musical expression of the period. By 1890 what was left was pedestrian naturalism à la Richard Strauss, or the artificial, sentimental *Weltanschauung* music of Gustav Mahler. By 1933 there were no longer any achievements of significance in this sphere and it is quite impossible to define the purpose of a symphony. So a really progressive composer will have to realize that this is a completely archaic art form, which should no longer be employed. Why continue the useless? We are witnessing a new blossoming and predominance of vocal music following the instrumental era of the nineteenth century. Instrumental music will play an increasingly subordinate and insignificant role in music. A solution to the music crisis emanating from purely instrumental music can't be found. The experiences of the last twenty years demonstrate this quite clearly. Modern composers have tried almost everything and the result is complete anarchy. The composer today depends only on his own personal recipe and his own taste. If this would guarantee a high musical culture, then there would be nothing against it. But since it inherently helps to produce barbarism and decay it is harmful. There were periods of great styles in the history of music, which were generally considered obligatory. As everybody knows it is often not easy to distinguish between an early Beethoven, Haydn or Mozart, without an exact analysis. Certain cadences were generally accepted as well as certain formal methods, such as the employment of additional musical elements in the transition, or as the development or the recapitulation. Despite all these generally accepted elements of form, the composers were not uniform; each possessed individuality.

Modern music will only exist when there is a new modern style which is obligatory for all and useful to society. At a time when modern music no longer has a public but is only promoted privately a composer can do as he likes. He can compose like Czerny and with a few false basses write a *"Book of Exercises for non-Dexterity."* He can copy Brahms with the twelve tone technique or sit on top of the piano declaring he is expressing his innermost soul. Since these three methods are as useless as they are unsalable the difference is minute. We find the same sort of anarchy in aesthetics. Today there are no aesthetic standards in music, for the difference between beautiful and ugly has become a matter of personal taste and experience. A modern type of composer must take note of that. The terms "beautiful" or "not beautiful" which played such an important role fifty years ago are out of date. They no longer say anything about the value and therefore must be replaced by the new "useful" and "useless." Many fellow musicians believe the only criterion is good or bad music. That sounds quite reasonable. Unfortunately, however, it is difficult today to agree on what is good and what is bad music. Some composers consider Stravinsky primitive, others consider Schönberg obsolete. There are a number of very talented modern composers, whose composing is technically bad from a certain point of view. Careless part writing, lack of artistry in the form, inability in the counterpoint. Yet there are others who will defend these composers, maintaining they intended to so write and it was not done out of ignorance, but to achieve certain "effects." Unfortunately, the terms "good" and "bad" alone are no longer adequate as criteria, nor yet the terms "modern" and "old-fashioned." But when we combine these criteria with the new criteria of "useful" and "useless" we will make better headway, especially if we go one step further and ask "useful for whom?" Technical standards among modern composers are bad, though generally not yet admitted. Among the best of them we often find only mannerisms instead of originality, style imitation instead of style, superficial tricks in place of fundamental technical workmanship. Anyone looking at what you might call a polyphonic work of a talented young composer would find little counterpoint, merely an imitation of it, or the use of certain counterpoint mannerisms. So today the terms "good" and "bad" must be applied with the greatest of care and in any case only in connection with "useful" or "useless."

The new type of composer will also have to learn that the crisis in modern music has been brought about mainly by the growth in technical devices. The radio, gramophone records and sound film have created a completely new situation. The concert compared with sound film is just as old-fashioned as the mailcoach compared with the airplane. Sound film and radio are destroying the old forms of music listening for there is a big difference between listening to a symphony at a concert or on the radio. There is a glaring contradiction between classical music and the modern means of production. Take a simple experiment—if you turn on the radio in a car driving along the street of a big city then you will realize that classical music does not fit the modern way of life. It requires a passive listener who is easily affected and who can shut off his thinking. The technique of composing classical music is dependent on this and arose because of it. If listened to over the radio or in a film many of the formal devices seem antiquated. For instance, the principle of recapitulation, of the development, indeed the whole sonata form itself. Sound film is making the masses unaccustomed to listening to music in the abstract but accustomed to seeing pictures of real life while they hear music. So a more realistic type of listener is arising in contrast to the old idealist concert-goer. This is a very interesting process. It is not altered by the fact that the film industry is helping to produce a barbaric condition in culture and that it is a political and moral device for blunting the intellect of the masses. Whether film will become a wonderful art form for mankind or a sordid commodity is a question of power, that is to say, a political question and not an aesthetic-cultural one. The sound film will also decisively change the state of instrumental music. The first experiments have been made to produce music synthetically on the film sound track. The sound chart of the composer's score is copied onto the film track. It sounds adventurous, but it has already been done. It is known how the tone A looks graphically on the film track and this graphic sign can be changed back again into music. The manual labor of the musician is thus replaced by the machine; this will lead to a complete revolutionizing of techniques of composing. But this means the composer can make himself absolutely independent of the inadequacies of the instruments and musicians. The conductor, the virtuoso and the instrumentalist will become superfluous. The result will be a still greater mass poverty among musicians, if the present form of society is not changed by then. It will not take too long, if we think of the short time that it took for the sound film to develop. Music-making by man will then have a new function, it will be for the music-lover and the amateur. (Just as the train, the car and the plane have not made walking or rambling disappear.) Great music will be put directly by the composer onto the apparatus; with the help of technicians, but no longer of "artists." (There will no longer be problems about the tempi or the rendering.) These are the material fundamentals and prerequisites for a new style in music.

It is not possible in such a brief exposition to enlarge on such problems systematically. They can only be touched on, so to speak. Nevertheless, from what has already been stated it is clear along what lines the new type of modern composer should think in order to arrive at a new musical practice. What are our main difficulties? Certain social situations have produced certain musical forms, that is, they produce a certain musical diction. If the material productive forces of a society develop at a quicker speed than the music, then music will lag behind and a contradiction will arise between it and society. With modern composers it is as though they find themselves in an airtight room, where there is no possibility of solving even the smallest technical problem. (All these struggles for a new technique and new aesthetics expire without showing any result. There are no victors any more, only the vanquished.)

Even if modern composers were of one mind at least on some questions, another type of man with a rough voice and hard hands would appear, bang on the table and demand, "For whose benefit?" And that is the main question.

In order to check the decay of music and to find a new technique, a new style and thus a new circle of listeners, the modern composer will have to leave his airtight room and find his place in society. It is not a question of sentimentality and kindheartedness but a question of music.

The modern composer must change *from a parasite into a fighter*. In the interests of music we must ask ourselves: What social attitude is the most useful? Once we have realized that the present form of society has produced musical barbarism, then we must try to change it. However, that is a very difficult matter, not easily achieved. We cannot conduct such struggles alone, but must form an alliance with those sections of the people who suffer under this order of society and who are combating it. That is an alliance of the progressive intellectuals, scholars, doctors, engineers, artists and the working class. The composer must understand once and for all that this alliance alone will provide the guarantee of bringing order into the chaos in music. This path is long and difficult, but in the interests of music it must be taken. It is also a question of character for there is a difference between a weakling, a futile dreamer (and whoever is futile is also harmful), or a modern man, a realist, who thinks and fights for his cause. In these times of mankind's great battles for a new world musicians should not desert the field. Let us join the struggle on the side of truth against falsehood. Then we will best serve our cause, the cause of modern music.

Source: *Einiges über die Lage des modernen Komponisten,* Typescript, Hanns Eisler Archives.
EGW III/1, pp. 362–69.
This was probably written in connection with Eisler's classes at the New School for Social Research, New York, where he lectured on "The Crisis in Modern Music," and which was intended for publication in *New Music,* a New York periodical. A shortened version appeared in English translation in *Daily Worker,* New York, Dec. 5, 1935, under the heading, "The Composer in Society."

The Crisis in Music
1935

The existence of a crisis in music today is by no means realized by all musicians and music lovers, or if realized not openly admitted. In fact, most average concert audiences, composers and critics, know nothing of such a crisis. The very speed, however, at which styles in serious music have been changing, the constant abandonment of innovations which had been hailed only a moment before, the very experimental nature of these innovations and the simultaneous existence of completely heterogeneous styles show that in practice the crisis is real and effective, even though a theoretical analysis has yet to be made.

That a crisis in music exists is no cause for wonder. It would be strange indeed if there were no such crisis.

In our social system music is undoubtedly produced as a luxury. When poverty increases to the extent it has today this luxury takes on a provocative character.

The question of whether music can take on a new social function becomes increasingly urgent.

In an apparently similar situation of general poverty in the year 500 B.C. the Chinese philosopher Me-Ti definitely decided against music. He said, "The fact that the people have been urged to make use of musical instruments has resulted in three disadvantages: the hungry are not fed, the cold are not clothed and the weary are not rested. If the scholars and nobles of the empire seriously wish to improve the people's welfare and remove all conditions of distress they will have to prevent and forbid music wherever it is practised."[1]

Shall we now draw the same conclusions as Me-Ti? In

a number of theses to follow, the possibilities for a way out will be examined.

I. The present-day crisis in music is but a part of the great economic crisis which is shaking the whole world and which has caused serious functional disturbances in every sphere of cultural life. The crisis in music can only be overcome to the extent that music itself takes part in solving the world-wide social crisis.

II. Composers, irrespective of the purpose for which they believe they are producing music, must become aware of the social function for which their music is being used. If they free themselves of all prejudices they will discover that regardless of their intentions, their music plays a great part in what can only be described as trade in narcotics.

The opinion is frequently heard that music by its very nature is not able to effect changes in the social life of man. However, it must be pointed out that this opinion has only arisen out of a peculiar practice over the last hundred years and previously was seldom voiced.

The history of Chinese music, of European music in the Middle Ages and of our own time shows that music has attempted again and again, more or less consciously, to play a part in social life.

If a composer today claims that his music has no social or political function, he merely reveals his ignorance of these functions.

III. Many musicians may wonder why they should suddenly be placed on the level of dealers in narcotics, after they have worked so unremittingly to carry on the traditions of classical music. For this in its time served a high and noble social function. It should be pointed out to them that the great music of Orlando di Lasso, of Bach or Beethoven is today being used for social functions in absolute contradiction to the original intentions of their composers. Think, for example, of how Hitler Germany uses Beethoven's "Eroica" symphony. In fact, music not only serves certain social functions, but allows of a change in these functions, so that it is then made to serve an aim different than that for which it was written.

IV. In changing the function of music why does society today direct it toward music that intoxicates and drugs the senses?

The present crisis has only increased the desire for such pacifiers and intoxicants which has arisen out of the peculiar circumstances of life under capitalism. If the masses want art to be intoxicating, or at least accept it, it is because they are seeking a psychological substitute for activities and experiences of which they are deprived through their position in society.

V. But in the same hopeless social situation the most advanced sections of the proletariat set up various organizations to take up the struggle for a radical change in the capitalist order of society. Only by participating in this struggle can music combat the causes that have led to a crisis in its own sphere.

VI. Participation in this struggle, the greatest that mankind has yet been engaged in, means nothing less than a total change in the functions of music, that is to say, we must strive to replace the old functions by new social functions. Instead of trying to bring about a state of psychic stupefaction or chaotic excitement in the listener, music must endeavor to clarify the consciousness of the most advanced class, the working class, and must attempt to influence the practical actions of the audience.

The following is a practical outline of what a change in the functions of music will mean for the composer:

VII.

Old function *Predominance of instrumental music*	New function *Predominance of vocal music*
The small musical forms for one or more instruments:	The small musical forms for one or more instruments:
sketches, character pieces, children's pieces reflecting the mood of the composer, perhaps also including formal innovations, études for development and exhibition of technical skill.	as opportunities for testing material and as training in logical-musical thinking.
The larger musical forms	The larger musical forms
sonata, quartet, orchestral suite, symphony: as expression of philosophy or of religious aspirations. Also as an exposition of "pure" forms. Spontaneous development of musical material (concerto-fashion and *spielfreudig*). Place: concert hall.	[sonata, quartet, orchestral suite, symphony:] as testing material for types of *Lehrstuecke* (didactic pieces), film music etc. Also as *Gebrauchsmusik* for political meetings, further, for the destruction of conventional musical concepts. Place: concert hall.
In film: as illustration, mood-painting.	*In film:* as musical commentary.
Songs: performed by a specialist in the concert hall to passive listeners. Subjective-emotional.	*Mass songs, songs of struggle:* sung by the masses themselves on the streets, in workshops or at meetings. Activating.

Ballads:
sentimental or heroic content. Mostly dealing with heroes.

Ballads:
containing social criticism often interspersed with ironic quotations of conventional music.

Choral songs:
as a mechanical transposition of the expression of an individual into a collective body, e.g. a solo song sung by a chorus of one hundred people *"I* cannot explain my sadness ..."

Choral songs:
workers' choir undertakes the teaching of mass songs and fighting songs to the audience.

Polyphonic choral pieces:
(see choral song)

Polyphonic choral pieces:
make possible the learning and presentation of theoretical sayings. Create models for didactic pieces.

Oratorio:
presenting religious material from the old or new testament, or material from classical narrative works.
Large musical form, sometimes, however, only a collection of lyrical pieces.

Didactic pieces:
make use of ballads, instrumental interludes and polyphonic choral pieces, also of independent theatrical productions.

Opera, operetta:
using the same musical form as in the oratorio, but weakened by the necessity to achieve theatrical effects.

Opera, operetta:
social criticism, depicting the social mores, destruction of conventional operatic effects.

Theater music:	*Theater music:*
atmospheric and illusion-producing. Not independent.	independent element as musical commentary.
The composer:	*The composer:*
as a personality. Individual style.	as a specialist, mastering several styles of composing.
The interpreter:	*The interpreter:*
has the character of one who merely delivers.	has the character of a consumer.

VIII. At performances of classical music the historical character of the music should be stressed to prevent socially harmful uses. This can easily be achieved by interpolating historical commentaries and musicological explanations into the program.

IX. A change in the social function of music offers the only possibility of raising musical standards and of developing the new methods.

The attempt of some modern composers to reach new strata of listeners by artificially lowering standards, while retaining the old narcotic function, is no solution.

X. The decisive criterion of the "social function" must be added to the criteria of "invention," "technical skill" and "feeling." Progress means not only the introduction of new technical methods, but the introduction of new technical methods serving new social functions.

Source: Article published by Downtown Music School, New York City, 1936, No. 1 of a series.

EGW III/1, pp. 370–75, under the title, *Gesellschaftliche Umfunktionierung der Musik.*

This is the text of a lecture given by Eisler on December 7, 1935, at a symposium and concert on the subject of "The Crisis in Music," at Town Hall, New York City.

Eisler was a faculty member of the Downtown Music School, which belonged to the American Music League, a "national organization for the advancement of music and for the maintenance of culture against war, fascism and censorship," as stated on the cover of Eisler's brochure.

1 The quotation from the tract, *The Damnation of Music* by Me-Ti, was often, even freely, quoted by Eisler and relying on his memory with incorrect date. The Chinese philosopher (497-381 B.C.) spoke in the interests of the working people against the division of society into nobles and lower orders, which Confucian teachings defended.

From My Practical Work
On the Use of Music in Sound Film
1936

There is little theory and inadequate practice in the use of music in sound film. That is a pity, for its most effective use is still not understood.

My work as a sound film composer began very early in Germany. In 1927 Dr. Bagier, the manager of the small and unknown Triergon Company, asked Paul Hindemith and myself each to compose a small film for the music festival in Baden-Baden. In those days sound recording apparatus was still very primitive. I well remember how Masolle (one of the inventors of the Tobis system) exhorted me in a paternal manner to avoid certain musical phrases. He named a whole list of things I was to avoid. Otherwise, he said, I could do as I like.

I was given the following job to do. With the aid of a rather inferior new invention, Blum's synchronizing apparatus, I was to "underline" all the "rhythms" in an abstract film by Ruttmann.[1] I must confess it seems idiotic to me today. (Hindemith composed music to *Felix der Kater,* where the underlining of the rhythm of the film had an excellent humorous effect.) Considering the state of film music at that time, it is not surprising that I was given such an assignment. A film composer was considered clever and useful if he understood how to "illustrate" the action of the film. If a machine was shown on the screen, the music had to whir, if a man was walking along the street, the music had to walk etc.

This principle of illustrating was supplemented by "sentimental" and "picturesque" music. The "sentimental" was used to make the sorrow of a lover more sorrowful by means of appropriate music. The "picturesque" were those abominable pieces of music which when green pastures were shown fell into a detestable sobbing, or became angry to suggest the roaring sea. The invention of sound film brought about a crisis in this type of film music. Since the sound film itself reproduced all the noises and sounds, the film "illustrator" became superfluous. However, in general, he was retained because music is effective and one didn't want to do without it. Today there is a certain anarchy in this sphere. One of the most deplorable results of this anarchy being so-called background music.

The dubbing of music over the dialogue is a method as bad as the old film "illustrator" with his card index of shots. The sound film raises new problems for the composer. I tried to solve some of these problems like this. In 1930 I worked with Granovsky on his film *Lied vom Leben*[2] (The Song of Life). Here for the first time I made use of a ballad in a non-naturalistic way. The birth of a child was shown in the film and the picture of the baby was accompanied by a ballad, depicting all the things that await a child. This gave Granovsky the idea of showing the same things in the film as well. And so music and film depicting all the horrors of this world resulted in a combination of picture and sound which at that time created considerable interest. It was fundamentally different from the method in which songs were usually introduced into films. (This method was often copied later on.)

In the same year I worked together with Victor Trivas on the film *Niemandsland* (No Man's Land). Victor Trivas is a highly talented director with great understanding of how to work together with a composer. Of the instances in which we succeeded to employ music and picture in an original way, I would like to quote just one: the beginning of the war. A workman says good-bye to wife and child— on the way to the barracks we see depressed men accompanied by their wives. Martial music starts very softly, gradually increasing until it reaches a fortissimo. While this music is played good-natured and anxious men turn into ferocious warriors. I believe that with this example we were very successful in showing the stultifying and narcotic effect of martial music.

Another use of martial music was shown by the director Karl Grune and myself in the film *Abdul Hamid*[3]. One scene shows Abdul Hamid (Fritz Kortner) beating a soldier because of his slovenly bearing, which is accompanied by the "seductive" sounds of the Hymn to the Sultan. I based myself on the supposition that a patriotic song is best illustrated by the mishandling of one of the singers of such a song.

In the film *Kuhle Wampe*[4], directed by Dudow, dwellings of poor people were shown. These very calm pictures were counterpointed with extremely energetic and stimulating music, which suggested not only pity for the poor, but at the same time provoked protest against their condition.

When Jacques Feyder was discussing the scenario of the film *Le grand jeu* with me, I suggested that a large-scale music piece should counterpoint the mass scene showing Foreign Legionnaires invading the prostitutes' quarter of an African garrison town, instead of the usual marmelade-marmelade music. Thus we achieved a more colorful and lifelike presentation than would have been possible with a so-called naturalistic one.

In the film *Komsomol (Song of Heroes)* which I made in Moscow and Siberia with Joris Ivens, we successfully combined sound and picture, contrasting original folk songs with modern music. A young peasant from a primitive Siberian tribal people (whose songs I had used at the beginning of the film) walks through the new socialist industrial town of Magnitogorsk for the first time. This walk was accompanied by a large-scale instrumental piece, whose distinctive character tried to make clear that building a foundry industry there was synonymous with the fight for a new way of life.

These are only a few of my experiences in film work, but they led me to the following conclusions.

The naive illustrative method is chiefly suitable for humorous or grotesque films. Walt Disney developed this method in the Silly Symphonies to the highest degree. In serious feature films this method is bound to fail in most cases; it reduces music to a secondary ineffective appendage. A new way of using vocal and instrumental music is above all to set the music against the action in the film. That means that the music is not employed to "illustrate" the film, but to explain it and comment on it. That may sound abstract, but my experience has shown that large sections of the film can be made much more effective by this method, and indeed effective in a popular sense. This method will also be necessary when seeking a new form for the musical comedy film and the film opera. The material prerequisites for a good film are that in preparing the scenario, the composer should be drawn in as music consultant from the beginning so that the music has the right function in the construction of the plot and the working out of the scenes. How much unnecessary work could be saved.

Further the producer and director should engage a qualified musician. I believe that modern composers have already proved their worth over popular composers, who for the most part, have their music orchestrated and arranged by run-of-the-mill arrangers. Film requires the best experts. A qualified composer is also able to write simple music, superior to that of the routine arranger. You can still see good films with poor music abominably orchestrated. It is high time that directors consider the quality of film music with the same seriousness they give to the problems of the sound film.

Source: *Aus meiner Praxis*, Typescript, Hanns Eisler Archives.
EGW III/1, pp. 383–86.
This article was written for and published by the London magazine, *World Film News*, No. 5, 1936.

1 The film referred to was called *Opus III* by Walter Ruttmann (1888–1942), one of the leading exponents of the socio-critical avant-garde and of *Neue Sachlichkeit* (Anti-Romanticism) in German films in the twenties.

2 Eisler composed *Anrede an ein neugeborenes Kind* (Address to a Newborn Child), lyrics by Walter Mehring, for the film, *Das Lied vom Leben* (The Song of Life).

3 The film *Kuhle Wampe* (1931–32) was the joint work of Bertolt Brecht (scenario), Hanns Eisler (music) and Slatan Dudow (director). It was the climax of the early proletarian films in Germany, both from the ideological point of view through the presentation of people in relation to the process of the revolutionary struggles of the time, but also because of its unusual dramaturgy: a combination of acting, reportage and impressions, together with commentary and contrapuntal music, which has its own independent value.

4 Eisler composed the music to *Le grand jeu* in Paris in spring 1934, and to *Abdul Hamid* in London in January 1935.

Letter to Bertolt Brecht

dear brecht,

this is the second letter that i am writing today and the second song that i am sending off. i think it is good. the effect lies in the fact that the music is terribly vulgar and nasty. it must be sung by a fat, blousy old hag with remains of titian beauty. it is easy to sing musically, but difficult to put over. very free in tempo. i have written these two songs for a single piano at the moment. the arranger should arrange them for two pianos in real cabaret style. the blues character must come out in the first song and the second song must have a street song character. both of these pieces are very different from the rest of the music and will probably introduce a bit of fun into the grim affair. i hope the texts will be translated in a way that will also bring out a certain humor in the words.

i'd also like to mention that in the song i am enclosing, the main motive from *Tristan und Isolde* by richard wagner has been used as accompaniment, for the masters should always be honored where it is necessary,

sincerely,
Eisler

Source: Copy, Hanns Eisler Archives.
EGW III/6 (in preparation).
Eisler wrote this letter from London to Brecht in Denmark, probably in October 1936.
The correspondence refers to the music to Brecht's satirical

play, *Die Rundköpfe und die Spitzköpfe* (The Round-Heads and the Pointed-Heads). The première was to be Nov. 4, 1936 in Copenhagen. In the letter Eisler means the two numbers, *Lied eines Freudenmädchens* (Song of a Loose Girl) and *Kuppellied* (Coupling Song). The music consists of 14 vocal numbers in all with accompaniment for a small instrumental group.

On a Concert for the
International Brigade in Spain
1937

When I called on Ludwig Renn in his quarters in Madrid he said, "A good thing you are here. You must organize a concert for us tomorrow. I sent out a warrant for you some time ago, didn't you receive it?" He rummaged among his papers and handed me a sheet of paper on which was written:

> Warrant for Hanns Eisler.
> Comrade Eisler, where are you now
> At the pole, in New York or in Moscow?
> Compose this for us we beg of you
> For us it's too hard
> For you it's fun to do.
> Straightaway send us the compositiona
> To Madrid and also to Barcelona!

Naturally, I wanted to organize a concert, but it wasn't so easy. The Brigade had just come from the front line and was going off the same night to the town of X, a few hours distant from Madrid. There was neither the time nor the opportunity to hunt out professional artists, nor was it quite so simple to put a program together. But Renn was used to bigger difficulties than that and calmed me down. "We'll simply write some new poems," he said, "and you can compose them straightaway. You can follow us to X tomorrow, we'll get a hall ready for you. In the morning you can teach the volunteers the songs and afterwards at five o'clock in the afternoon that'll be our concert." Renn took his writing pad and started to work out song texts from old notes for poems. He gave the first to

128

me as soon as he had finished it and I started composing. We were often interrupted by orderlies and by the comings and goings caused by a battalion that was moving off. I very much admired Renn's calmness as he went on making up verses between military dispositions, discussing phrases here and there with me. After working two hours I went off to my quarters with four new songs and made fresh copies.

The next day I met the battalions in X and a memorable morning began. In a little restaurant the battalion secretary, a woman, was typing the stencils of the new program. This was immediately rolled off in a few hundred copies, so that everyone attending the concert could have a printed program with the new texts for joining in the singing. From the various companies comrades who could sing began coming in to report. We rehearsed right up until the concert was due to begin.

With the Spanish comrades I rehearsed the new *Marsch des fünften Regiments* which I had composed in Madrid to a Spanish text. The chief of the French battalion, Dumont, sent me a French text which I rehearsed with the French comrades. Austrian comrades had even got hold of an accordion. With the German comrades we rehearsed the song 7. *Januar*. A group of Jewish volunteers needed me to accompany them in a recital of some of their wonderful folk songs.

In the afternoon one of the most unusual concerts that I have ever attended began punctually at five o'clock.

On the stage were the volunteers who were to sing. Some of the wounded were still in bandages. Volunteers and Spaniards were sitting in the auditorium. The fierce desire for some form of cultural life, even the simplest, was shattering. And that one must really understand. The volunteers had endured tremendous hardships and were about to face still bigger ones. Coming from the front they wanted to give vent to all the onerous and wonderful experiences they had encountered. They wanted to get together with other battalions of various nationalities and fraternize with them.

It was a stirring performance. The singing was not beautiful, their voices were hoarse from the extreme cold in the trenches. But their singing was alive and they sang with enthusiasm. That's how the peasants must have sung their songs of rebellion in the peasant wars, how the Taborites[1] must have sung, and how the *Marseillaise* must have sounded for the first time. For me as a composer it was a most instructive evening, for it demonstrated once again how necessary music is and how important it can be in the great struggles for a new world.

Source: Typescript, Hanns Eisler Archives.
EGW III/1, pp. 395–96.
This article was written in November 1937 in Prague, probably intended for *Ilustrovaný Časopis*, published in the same month under the heading, *Koncert na frontě*.

5,000 German anti-fascists fought in the International Brigade in Spain. The author, Ludwig Renn, formerly an army officer and member of the German nobility, joined the Communist Party in 1928. From 1936–37 he was the head of the Thälmann Battalion and Chief-of-Staff of the XIth International Brigade.

In January 1937 Eisler visited the Spanish front, where he composed *Das Lied vom 7. Januar,* words by Ludwig Renn, the *Marsch des fünften Regiments* and the song *No pasarán,* words to the latter 2 songs by Herrera Petere.

[1] Taborites were members of the radical party of the Hussites (15th century).

Labor, Labor Movement and Music

*Speech to the Choir
of the International Ladies'
Garment Workers Union
1938*

When I speak to you about labor, or the labor movement and music I do so with a certain responsibility, for I must not only give you some ideas, but must also show you how they can be practical and progressive. If we are going to speak about music we must first make a general outline of the specific situation in musical life today. When doing this perhaps it is better to omit abstract philosophical formulations, and be concrete and realistic.

Let us imagine that we are interviewing different types of musicians and music lovers. Perhaps their answers will be illuminating.

Let us put the following question to any famous conductor (and I know a number of them), "What is the purpose of music in your opinion and from your point of view as a conductor, and whom do you believe is served by your work?" The usual answer will be, "Music has no special purpose. The purpose of music lies in itself. My job is to give the people beauty, and to try and give them as much as possible."

That sounds all very well, but is it the truth? Does that really serve the people, or does the typical concert conductor not really serve a certain small section of the people—the wealthy upper class? And when a conductor performs serious classical or modern music on the radio, are the people, the working class and the petty bourgeoisie really able to understand such music? Was music always written without a particular purpose? The answer to all these questions is, no.

First of all, music for the sake of music, or art for art's sake is a very young slogan, not more than a hundred years old. The great masters in the history of music never used such slogans. For example, Johann Sebastian Bach said of himself, "My duty is to serve the Lord and the Church with my music."[1] His feelings were not so much those of an artist as those of an artisan or preacher. Beethoven was thoroughly influenced by his times, the era of the great French Revolution. If you read Wagner's theoretical writings from 1848, you will find that they are directly antagonistic to slogans such as "art for art's sake."

What is the reason for the present disavowal of the attitude of the truly great masters and their traditions? We will find the answer if we examine the second part of the conductor's statement, that he wants to serve the people. We know that today very few people really understand and find pleasure in serious classical or modern music.

Of course, I realize that some of the great works enjoy a certain popularity, but that is mainly among the intellectuals in the big cities. However, New York, Chicago, San Francisco, Los Angeles and Boston are not the United States alone. When broadcasting companies send out questionnaires on the program wishes of their listeners, 99 percent answer, "Give us more entertainment music and less symphonies." If classical music has so small a basis, what chance is there for serious modern music?

This is an important point. Why? Because a sound musical situation requires a constant flow of new musical works. Let us now question a modern composer, someone as well-known as Arnold Schönberg. He will certainly answer, "I am completely isolated. Very few people understand my music, perhaps a hundred or two." If we ask him why he continues to write under these abnormal conditions he will say, "I have to express myself, and perhaps in a couple of hundred years people will understand what I have written." Yet this is not only true of composers with world-wide reputations like Schönberg, every student who writes in a modern style, and every young composer is in the same terrible fix.

Was this always so? No, absolutely not. Beethoven and Wagner[2] were isolated for some years, but this dilemma did not endure the whole of their lifetime. And in the history of music there was never a period where all musical production was in such a predicament as it is today. What is wrong? Are modern composers not proficient? Are the people lacking in understanding? Again the answer is, no. Arnold Schönberg is an excellent composer and there are understanding people in all countries. But something is wrong. The disaster begins when you divide music into entertainment and serious categories. Ask the music critic of a well-known liberal newspaper in New York. Most likely he will answer, "My dear friend, this division has always existed. Don't worry about it. It has always been that some people have more appreciation of art than others. Don't take it to heart, my dear Mr. Eisler. Do you really think that Beethoven was understood by all the people of his time? Or Mozart? Certainly not."

In answer to this we could say to our friend the music critic, "But don't forget that now there are more practical opportunities for hearing and understanding music. Just think of the radio. But has the radio brought about any definite changes?" Again my answer is, no.

Summing up for the conductor, the composer and the critic, we can say, music today is in a crisis. And we, as the class-conscious political and artistic avant-garde, must say that this crisis is an expression of the deep economic and political world crisis.

One characteristic of this crisis in music is the division of entertainment and serious music. Is this not a very strange division? Must we be entertained only by the cheapest musical rubbish and must we look serious and behave like snobs when listening to serious classical music? Again history can teach us. In the history of music we seldom find any circumstance where music was a direct and natural expression of and for the people without any restrictions or difficulties. Only in primitive society, for example among the American Indians, or in ancient oriental culture, or in the ancient Germanic, Roman and Celtic societies, do we find an unbroken unity of sacred and secular music. But in the Middle Ages we find a special differentiation between church music and popular music. This division does not entirely correspond with our division of serious and entertainment music. In the fifteenth and sixteenth centuries we find a highly developed church music, a very refined music for the aristocratic courts and for the wealthy merchant class in the new bourgeois cities in Italy, France and the Netherlands. Next to these more specialized forms of art music we find typical "useful" music of and for the ordinary people, mainly dance music and folk songs.

We must remember that a musician like Bach served both the church and the aristocracy. There was certainly a constant connection between this art music and folk music. Church music often used folk songs and vice versa: the people often sang church melodies. At that time folk music had a real cultural basis and tradition. From earliest times primitive manual labor and craftsmanship were connected with music. The purpose of this music was to organize primitive cooperative labor—sailing, fishing, farming and other crafts. Some festival and religious songs testify by their words that they were directly connected with this primitive labor. Further, we must not forget that until the seventeenth century the church was open to everybody and was a decisive factor in cultural musical life in general.

I won't go into further detail here about historical material. However, you may be interested in an example of a familiar song. I am sure you all know the famous "Volga Boatmen's Song."[3] You can hear it in any White Russian tea room or cabaret. Former so-called noblemen tenderly remember the good old times when they could cheerfully kick a peasant in the pants. But was this song always an expression of the ideas of these filthy noblemen-bandits?

No. It is an old and revered song. It was actually used by boatmen on the Volga River, not only to express themselves, but also to organize their work of pulling the boats upstream. Obviously when so many men have to pull a heavy boat they have to use their force at the same time, that is to say, in a definite rhythm provided by the song. Otherwise they would be unable to move the boat or to use their labor force most economically. Later on, this song became a real folk song and was used for many kinds of manual labor. Let us go farther. Suppose a smart businessman hears the boatmen singing and likes it. He thinks that song may mean business. He hires some carpenters to build benches on the river banks; he then sells tickets to the ladies of rich city merchants to hear for the first time the original Volga boatmen singing the original "Volga Boatmen's Song." And the beautiful ladies enjoy the song very much.

As you know, generally speaking, art and music today are the prerogatives of rich ladies. They come to listen again and again, and the "Volga Boatmen's Song" is a great hit. But after a time the women say, "Today the performance was not very good, in fact, it was rather poor. Yet last Monday the performance was first class. Divine! What has happened?" They ask the boatmen and the answer is curious. The boatmen say, "Today the boat was quite light, it was not loaded. But last Monday we had to pull very heavy stones. We had to work very hard and so we sang with all our might."

This is not meant as a joke. You can certainly see the difference between music today and the old folk music culture, where the people sang for themselves and not for listeners. In genuine old folk music no difference existed between entertainment and serious music. In old art music, let us say that of Mozart, no differences existed. In his operas, *The Magic Flute* and *The Seraglio,* the music is both serious and entertaining.

The present differentiation began with the Industrial

Revolution at the beginning of the nineteenth century. What did the Industrial Revolution mean for society in general? It meant the birth of a new type—the industrial worker. The industrial worker lost his simple rural culture, he lost his old mores and habits and he lost his craftsmanship and his small property. These were all taken from him by force, in order to make of him a proletarian who had nothing to sell but his labor power. All this occurred as the technique of the division of labor progressed. Read the reports of the factory inspectors of the 1840's, 1850's and 1860's and you will realize the dehumanizing, degenerating and humiliating effects the Industrial Revolution had on the working class. In these reports there are the most horrible details about child labor, female labor, killing exploitation, the unlimited powers of the employers and the helplessness of the employees. At that time, the bourgeoisie grew in strength and reached the heights with geniuses like Beethoven, Goethe, Byron, Shelley and Balzac. The worker was no longer a human being. On the one hand there was a glorious bourgeois culture, and on the other there were the uncultured faceless masses. But from these helpless masses, the vanguard, the industrial workers in magnificent cooperation with progressives of all professions, sought and found a way out of their condition. They became *class-conscious*. They discovered the economic reasons and the driving forces behind all these developments; and it was only a short time for the tremendous development from utopian socialist ideas to the scientific methods of Marx and Engels and the beginning of political organization.

I could go on talking about these things, but they belong more to a lecture on the history of the working class. But for us there is one interesting point: What did the Industrial Revolution do to music culture? It destroyed most of the old folk music. The explanation is simple. Factory workers cannot sing at work in the same way and for the same reasons as the Volga boatmen sang. The tempo and rhythm of their work is dictated by their machines and not by the workers themselves. Spontaneous music culture dies under such conditions. Two generations after the Industrial Revolution the majority of the population was without any music culture at all. And this is how the division between entertainment and serious music arose!

In order to understand serious music it is necessary to have a high general level of culture and to have a high standard of living. That is to say you must have time, money and education enough to be able to play at least one instrument; you must have a more or less theoretical training and a certain general knowledge of the fine arts, literature and so on. You must have the opportunity of hearing musical works again and again, you must learn to play them yourself. All this can make you a really proficient music lover and musical amateur. It is evident that all this is available only to the middle class or to the upper class. Without a similar social background and similar social conditions you are more or less helpless.

It is also true that the nineteenth century composer, the romantic composer, wrote for and expressed the sentiments of this section of society. Schumann, Chopin, Liszt, Brahms[4] and others were the musical lions of upper middle-class drawing rooms. The thousands of love songs and piano pieces were sung and played by the young *Daughters of the Industrial Revolution.*

In addition, by the nineteenth century, art music was no longer solely music for the social soirees of emperors, princes and noblemen, but for the first time became merchandise and a business. A hundred years before the Industrial Revolution a man like Bach was at one and the same time a servant of the church, servant of the court, composer, piano-, violin- and organ player, teacher of Latin, French and musical composition. He also printed some of his own works; he was a copyist and librarian for his church. He was not a romantic figure like Liszt, but a normal good citizen with twelve children.[5] The Industrial Revolution created the traveling music virtuoso, who was like a traveling salesman. The composer became a specialist, he was *only* a composer, like Beethoven. The music teacher became a specialist, the special music theoretician, like Albrechtsberger; he taught only theory, but was neither a virtuoso nor a composer. The music publisher also came into being, and thus also the owners of concert halls, which were formerly located in the castles of noblemen. Then came the concert manager, often the same person as the concert virtuoso. Later he became independent, a sheer businessman in music, buying and selling the "merchandise" music. The music historian also appeared, a new and often curious type. So we see that quite a number of new and special types developed and became involved in the break between serious and entertainment music; they took into their hands the process of distribution and merchandising, of the buying and selling of music as a commodity.

Despite these negative features, this development in the nineteenth century was a progressive one. On the one hand we find a number of very talented composers and virtuosi, on the other hand a new and highly cultivated type of listener and musical amateur. At that time no musical crisis existed in the form that it does today, although characteristic of the times around the year 1800 a musical crisis started. But this apparently relatively peaceful and normal picture is altered sharply if you consider not just the new organization of musical life, but the dreadful background of the overall social conditions at this period. In England where the earliest and most radical industrial revolution took place, 90 percent of the population lived in ignorance and cultural darkness. It leads us to say that the social conditions of the time were a fundamental danger to further cultural development.

What kind of music was practised and was necessary for the uncultured 90 percent? It had to be the kind of music which could be produced and consumed as quickly and cheaply as beer or gin, as glaring and as bad as the new factory-made clothes. But just as gin is not very healthy and just as cheap clothing is neither beautiful nor durable, so also was the new "entertainment" music. It was cheap, factory-made and without any cultural value. This music was only digestible for those bereft of any musical taste. One condition alone was necessary, that they were not deaf. Naturally, such music was not created by great masters, nor yet by the people themselves. It was by no means folk music of the old type. It was music watered down for the people by mere music merchants. Fourth- and fifth-rate composers were paid by these merchants to write this sort of false "popular" music, and publishing houses printed it—cheap music, cheap words on cheap paper—and sold it in the streets like newspapers or candy. The production of such music increased with the invention of mechanical musical instruments. As entertainment music of this kind increased, serious music decreased.

Today entertainment music has become so predominant on the radio and in films that it can be heard at any time of the day or night. If you turn on the radio, if you go to a restaurant for a glass of beer, you always hear such music.

What does this kind of music give the people? I ask you to answer this question. What does a big glass of whiskey give you? Nothing but a headache after a very short period of pleasure. If you drink too much you end up in hospital. In particular, if young people hear too much of this music they become mentally dull and disinterested in the real needs and potentialities of the working class.

Let us now turn to the present day, the period of an unprecedented musical crisis. Though the nineteenth century be the father of this musical crisis, we must nonetheless judge the child. The great economic crisis after the world war largely affected the middle classes as well as most professionals throughout the world. The younger generation, influenced by new conditions, with new habits and new standards prefers sport and films to concerts. In this country in particular serious music is promoted and sponsored only by wealthy women. Of course middle-class youth, students and intellectuals are to be found at the concerts, but that does not alter the general picture. If there were to be a very special, very peculiar earthquake which would swallow up only wealthy women, then on the following day conductors, singers, pianists and composers would be found on the bread lines. Although it is the wealthy who sponsor serious music, they no longer have a monopoly on understanding good music as had the middle class and the aristocracy in the eighteenth and nineteenth centuries. Today concert-going is mostly an opportunity for displaying dress, jewelry and snobbishness. The fashionable and handsome Stokowskis[6] are admired more than the musical compositions that these gentlemen try to conduct. Composers, conductors, singers and teachers must have close relationships with these wealthy women, whose sponsorship is not too wholesome. It is sometimes awful to see what parasites some artists become, rather than as free men making their talents responsible to the people. How can musical standards be maintained under such protective conditions? Let me give you some facts. The Metropolitan Opera is the wealthiest of its kind in the world. For about fifty years a number of wealthy families have supported the opera with large donations. How many of you have ever attended a Metropolitan Opera performance? I suppose half a dozen, or perhaps no one. Have you any knowledge of the great operatic works of Mozart, Beethoven, Handel or Wagner? You may even say that although the Metropolitan Opera does not serve the people directly, they are creating a fine opera tradition which someday may be of use to the country. But I must answer, no. Of course the technical standard of the orchestra is very high and they have some excellent singers. However, the conductors are not first class, only experienced and good routine musicians. Culturally the whole standard is rather low. Nothing is done to modernize the productions; the performances are not usually first class. The old operas are performed again and again in a routine way. This is not a cultural institution, it is a luxury club for snobs. Further, who selects the conductors? Wealthy women select wealthy conductors. Musical ability is of secondary importance. Who works out the concert programs? The same wealthy women work out rather bad programs. They are generally like round-trip express trains from Beethoven to Sibelius. Is anything done for modern American composers? No. Who is responsible for this? The wealthy women sponsors! Which class do these wealthy women represent? The bankers, manufacturers, merchants and department store owners. Can this class be a leading force in the musical life of the people? No. Who can help the people? The people!

There are few good concerts available to the people today. Except for some popular concerts, only the cheap trash of Broadway and Hollywood is offered. I don't consider jazz and swing entirely bad. Men like Duke Ellington and Benny Goodman are really talented musicians. But Duke Ellington makes his fortune in night clubs and his development as an artist is therefore handicapped. Benny Goodman, a very fine clarinetist, has made stupid and boring films in Hollywood and thus ruins his real craftsmanship. What is being offered to the people as musical fare? Songs like, *Bei mir bist du schön, Ti-pi-tin,* and similar stupidities. And I shudder to think of the thousands of sentimental love songs produced by Broadway and Hollywood. Some of you will say, that's harmless, that's just entertainment, don't worry. But as a musician I do worry, for I know all is poison, opium for the people. But what is the solution? Should the working people grow long beards and with great dignity attend only concerts of serious music? That is ridiculous and impossible.

Before I continue, let me say a few favorable words about the United States. I am happy to say that the administration in this country and President Roosevelt are *also* progressive in the sphere of culture. I think that a great deal of the WPA[7] work in the theater and in music is admirable. But can the Government provide the solution? That is impossible. A progressive government can certainly help the people. But that is only a temporary help and not a definite change. The main support for the people, I repeat, is the people themselves.

But who are the people? You are the people. Let me say something about your possibilities as a workers' choir. I believe that since your union has worked so successfully in the theatrical field you will also want to do something important in your field. To be frank, I have had no personal experience with your organization. I have never heard any of your performances; I don't know your conductor or your qualities as a choir, and I don't know what you sing. But I can tell you about some of the conclusions I have drawn from international experience. Of course, the United States is different from France, England, Germany, Switzerland, Austria before Schuschnigg and Hitler, Germany before Hitler, Czechoslovakia (I hope never to have to say "before Hitler"), Denmark, Jugoslavia and last but not least the Soviet Union.

I have lived and worked as a musician in all these countries. Perhaps some of my experiences may be of use to you. I have seen highly successful choral organizations like the excellent People's Front Choir in France with 250 voices and a similar organization in London under the leadership of Alan Bush. I have heard millions of people singing my songs on Red Square on the first of May in Moscow. But I have also seen and heard other workers' choral groups and I must confess that sometimes I was unable to tell whether they were alive or dead. What is the reason for this?

A weak workers' choir usually has no special line. They are neither fish nor fowl, neither bourgeois nor proletarian. They sing popular lyrical choral music. For example, in Germany they used to sing, *Wer hat dich, du schöner Wald,* a sentimental popular chorus by Mendelssohn. Or they sing some popular works by good composers. But mostly they sing cheap lyrical rubbish by fourth- or fifth-rate composers. Such music is not only boring to sing, but is intolerable to listen to. Most of these pieces were written at the end of the nineteenth century and before the war. They have nothing in common with great art, nor do they express real life today. Poor choirs also sing some folk songs, usually badly arranged for four-part choir. Finally, they also sing what we call in German *Tendenz* choruses, that is choruses with conscious social significance. In Germany, the Netherlands and in England many *Tendenz* choral compositions were written between 1890 and 1920. Some of these pieces are really excellent, but most of them sound rather old-fashioned today. I am sure you know such pieces. The words are usually innocuous and quite mild like: "Today we are struggling in the night, but we hope that tomorrow there will be light," or "Some day we shall be free."

The music is equally old-fashioned and so is the behavior and the concert performance of the choir. These good people work very hard for six months on such a program. They hire a hall, put on their Sunday best, stand with great dignity and solemnity on the stage, follow very carefully the indications of the conductor, and do what is called their best. The audience is usually made up of relatives of singers, fellow union members and other friends. But the whole atmosphere is funereal. So the question remains, "Who is dead?" Maybe progressive music. The program begins. First come a couple of folk songs, or rather something masquerading as folk songs. I am always horrified to hear a group of union workers, toughened by many class struggles singing, "La, la, la, la, la, la, laaaa, aaaa," or "I am so lonesome when I remember you."

After these wonderful songs comes the obligatory classical repertoire, two or three pieces by better composers. If the performance is not very good, no matter, the audience has heard better performances on the radio. Finally, the choruses with social significance are sung. With ramrod

143

stiffness and monotony you hear the promise that "Sometime the sun will shine again," or "Freedom, we love you."

Now and then the conductor has a friend or a wife who plays the violin or piano, or sings solo. And so a soloist appears on the program. Pieces like Liszt's "Love Dreams," with its arpeggios going up and down, or the "Sweet Kreisleriana" for violin; if he or she is a singer then you hear pieces like Grieg's "I love you," and certainly at the end "Laugh, Pagliacci."

The listeners are very polite and the concert ends peacefully with the presentation of a bouquet of flowers to the conductor—organized by the concert committee. And all this is the result of six months' hard work. I often ask myself, What do the singers do at the rehearsals, especially the second tenors and the second basses? oooooooooolalalalala-lalalalalaa.

The bass line itself is stupid, but perhaps they console themselves with the thought that the whole thing may not sound too bad. I am sure that after such a concert, an executive committee meeting is held and somebody asks why the audience was so small in number. "Too little publicity and not enough ticket selling," the chairman will say.

I'm not convinced, even if you used a machine gun to sell tickets. The chairman, I am sure, will want to know why so few people attend rehearsals. I can understand the feelings of the choir members, especially my good friends, the second basses. Frequently it is difficult to find a person under forty in such choirs. The reasons for this are all quite obvious.

We talked about the crisis in music a little while ago, of the division between entertainment and serious music. A concert of this kind has nothing to do with the crisis in music. Surely such a concert is neither entertaining nor serious music. It is merely a boring, meaningless, inartistic, an utterly dreary affair. However, half a century ago, this kind of concert would have been a sign of real progress for the working class, but today it means less than nothing.

Especially to the younger generation who prefer the movies, the radio and sport; and if they are politically minded they go to meetings, left theater groups and so on. But if a cultural organization cannot attract the youth then it is not fulfilling its function and will lose vitality.

What can such an organization do under these circumstances? If each member realizes that these difficulties are part of a more general crisis and of the specific social conditions of the working class, then a way out will be found more easily. Let me give you some suggestions:

1. The main question is the repertoire. This must be chosen so that it is both interesting for the audience and for the singers (last but not least for the second basses) and for each voice of the choir—rehearsing the pieces for six months. The music and words must be engaging and stimulating.

How can a repertoire of this kind be formed? The only way is close contact with modern progressive composers. I have told you about the dreadful situation of the modern composer, who is either isolated and starving or who lives as a parasite. But you can give him a new chance! And he will give you a new chance! This collaboration between the progressive working class and progressive composers is mutually beneficial. For a progressive choral group this cognizance is absolutely vital. Close contact with such a group carries a fresh wind to the composer, new ideas, opportunities for publication, in short, a new life.

In building a repertoire there must be the right balance between classical art music and modern music. One important point is to forget old-fashioned rigidity. A modern conductor or composer can easily find not only good classical pieces for you, but interesting new works by different modern composers from various countries. Then there are the folk songs of the fifteenth and sixteenth centuries and the marvelous madrigals of composers like Orlando di Lasso, Marenzio and numerous others of the highest level.

There is also abundant material in modern music of

class-conscious compositions from many countries, including the Soviet Union. Finally, you can ask modern composers to write new works for you.

But unfortunately such a concert consisting of short pieces would add up to a boring evening. Which brings me to suggestion number two.

2. Improved methods of organizing concerts:

To hell with all this old rigmarole and concert mannerisms! We have more important things to do. Choose a good narrator. Let him explain the numbers which are to be sung, not in a dry academic manner, but in the fresh, witty and lively spirit of the working class. That will be one step forward.

But again not sufficient. More is required if a concert is to be organized effectively. You must try to cooperate with other artistic working-class groups, such as actors, dancers, bands and so on. Your composers and poets must write bigger cantatas, musical plays with action and music in which the role of the chorus is the most important. The whole responsibility for the political and social context in this new production lies on your shoulders. Rehearsals will give you ample opportunity to control and discuss things.

3. Humor, pep and satire should be an important part of all your performances. People like jazz and swing, they can be used in your productions, but not in the corrupt manner of Hollywood and Broadway. Good modern music has rhythm, humor and vitality, and you must exploit it. To conclude, what is the most vital thing?

A good modern conductor and a good relationship with (and a little money for) your modern composers—and only the best are good enough for you! You must have the most talented young poets. All this is possible. Try it! Remember that the death of art is cheap sentimentality, empty bombast and vulgar imitations of folk songs. The absence of social significance also makes a piece dreary, especially in these hard times. In our art there must be the finest unification of entertainment, a highly developed technique, awareness, humor, good propaganda and social feeling. Cheapness and a boring quality are the most dangerous enemies of workers' art. May I make a practical proposal to you. With your strong union, you have special possibilities and special experiences. Try the following: with some actors, one good narrator and a young modern director, with a young modern poet and a composer you could easily produce a marvelous choral play. I will give you a tip–let us say the name of the choral play is "Our Story," a play based on the history of your union. I know its history and it is wonderful, from an artistic point of view as well. For example, there could be a choral number about a Jewish immigrant, sitting on his trunks on Ellis Island, seeing New York across the bay. Another scene could show the semi-illegal work of the union in its beginnings; the fights with gangsters, the death of a militant brother–the choir could sing an explanation to this. A number of scenes could follow, and for each scene you could project onto the screen the date and some lines explaining the historical situation. The choir should not try to act! In general it would be too difficult and not good enough. They should be sitting and stand up to sing their numbers. You could have a couple of actors and one or two solo singers. With the same amount of energy that you used to prepare a concert of the kind I have analyzed, you could prepare a fine performance, important for you and your audience, with stimulating rehearsals and an active organization behind you.

Is all this difficult to do? Yes and no! The beginning will not be easy, but you must take this way, the way of a progressive workers' choir. In these times of cultural barbarism and political danger we can observe a very interesting phenomenon. Capitalist culture is on the decline. It is your turn now to guard and re-create culture despite all those wealthy women.

Let me end on a personal note. I would like to express my gratitude to Messrs. Schaeffer and Liebmann for the opportunity of speaking to you. I hope that something of what I have said may be useful and I hope that soon I will be able to congratulate you on your first flop!

Source: *Labor, labor movement and music,* Typescript, Hanns Eisler Archives.
EGW III/1, pp. 414–28.
The original English text was edited for this book. Eisler delivered this lecture to the choir of the International Ladies' Garment Workers' Union in New York, a choir with a rich tradition, on June 25, 1938.

1 With a quotation attributed to Bach, namely, that it is his duty to serve the Lord and the Church through his music, Eisler meant neither the acceptance of the church as an institution, nor the justification for turning one's back on society. On the contrary Bach's religiosity was on a par with his humanist thinking. "He always composed for life, he fulfilled his commissions by writing for purposes which were vital and for particular circles of people ... In contrast to his predecessors, there is in Bach's works a humanizing of the content undreamt of up to that time." (Ernst Hermann Meyer, *Aufsätze über Musik,* Berlin 1957, pp. 16–17.)

2 Richard Wagner fought on the barricades during the bourgeois-democratic revolution of 1848–49 in Germany, and at that time wrote discourses such as, "Man and Existing Society," "Art and Revolution," and "The Art of the Future."

3 The "Volga Boatmen's Song," an old Russian work song, became well-known in Western Europe and America, especially through the dolled-up interpretation of the famous bass, Feodor Chaliapin.

4 Schumann, Chopin, Liszt and Brahms, indeed all endeavored to reach the lower classes with their music, but
the proletariat was still in the process of being formed and
lay outside their mental horizon. On the other hand, they
profited from the middle and upper strata of the bourgeoisie.

5 Bach had 20 children: 7 children from his first marriage,
4 of whom lived; from his second marriage 13 children, 7
of whom reached maturity.

6 By "Stokowskis" Eisler meant star conductors of the
kind characterized by Leopold Stokowski in the U.S.A.

7 WPA is the abbreviation for Works Progress Administration.

Fantasia in G-men
1947

This hearing is both sinister and ridiculous. This committee is not interested in any testimony I may give or in anything I can testify about. The only thing of any public importance about me is my standing as a composer. Although my reputation is international, I do not suppose that that fact makes my musical activities un-American. I would be delighted to spend as much time as this Committee will allow to lecture on musical topics, the only matters which I am qualified to speak about. I could then discuss, for example, the development technique of Beethoven's last sonatas and string quartets or analyze the art of the fugue. But I doubt that I have been called to further such cultural interests.

On the contrary, this Committee has called me only in order to continue its smear of me in the press, hoping that it will thereby intimidate artists throughout the country to conform to the political ideas of this Committee. This is the second time you have called me to testify, the first being before your subcommittee in Hollywood last May.

The interest you show in me is quite flattering. But it has no proper purpose. To prove this let me tell you about my activities in this country. I first came to the United States early in 1935 under the auspices of a British committee headed by Lord Marley, of the British House of Lords, to raise money for the children of German anti-Nazi refugees. I made a concert and lecture trip for two or three months. The subject of my lectures was the destruction of musical culture under Adolf Hitler. My lectures were in German and were translated to my audiences.

I returned to the United States in the fall of 1935 in order to accept a professorship of music at the New School for Social Research in New York City. There I taught theory of musical composition and counterpoint. At this time also there was produced on Broadway a musical play, *The Mother,* for which I had written the score. I left the United States early in 1936 to become musical supervisor and composer for the British International Pictures' production *Pagliacci.* I returned to the United States at the beginning of 1938 and resumed teaching music at the New School.

In May 1939, I went to Mexico City to become visiting professor of music at the State Conservatory. About September 1939, I again returned to teach at the New School. At this time I composed the score for a picture for the New York World's Fair.[1]

In October 1940, I was admitted to the United States as an immigrant on a non-quota visa as a professor of music. About that time the Rockefeller Foundation made a grant of $20,000 for me to direct in the New School a research project on the relation of modern music and the films. The results of this study appear in my book, entitled *Composing for the Films,* just published by the Oxford University Press. If the Committee is interested in my artistic beliefs and principles, I recommend that each member of the Committee read this book and study it very carefully.

In the last five years I have lived in Hollywood where I have written the music for eight motion pictures, including *None But the Lonely Heart, Hangmen Also Die, Spanish Main, Woman on the Beach* and *So Well Remembered.* I was also for a short time a professor of music at the University of Southern California.

During all this time I have also written numerous symphonic works for orchestra, chamber music and vocal music. My last performed compositions include a woodwind quintet, sonata No. 3 for piano, variations for piano, sonata for viola and piano, cantatas for alto, two clarinets, viola and cello, symphonia brevis for orchestra etc.[2] Many of my compositions have been recorded.

These, gentlemen, are my activities in the United States and I must suppose that these are what the Committee considers "un-American." Apparently you are not connoisseurs of music.

In the United States I have never engaged in political activities and was never a member of a political party. The Committee knows these things about me from its investigations and earlier hearing. Why then am I subjected to this fantastic persecution? Why has the Committee outdone itself to smear my name for over a year? Why has it made it difficult for me to earn my living? Why has the Committee induced the State Department to threaten unlawful action to prevent me from visiting Paris to compose the score for a French production of *Alice in Wonderland?*

The answers to all these questions are very simple. I am accused of being the brother of Gerhart Eisler, whom I love and admire and whom I defend and will continue to defend. Does the Committee believe that brotherly love is un-American? More important, the Committee hopes that by persecuting me it will intimidate many other artists in America whom it may dislike for any one of various unworthy reasons. The Committee hopes to create a drive against every liberal, progressive and socially conscious artist in this country, and to subject their works to an un-Constitutional and hysterical political censorship. It is horrible to think what will become of American art if this Committee is to judge what art is American and what is un-American.

This is the sort of thing Hitler and Mussolini tried. They were not successful and neither will be the House Committee on Un-American Activities.

Source: *Fantasia in G-men* in *New Masses*, New York, Oct. 14, 1947.
EGW III/1, pp. 521–23.

This statement appeared in German translation in *Tage-buch*, Vienna, Nov. 14, 1947. In *New Masses* it was introduced with the following: "And now Hanns Eisler! After hounding this great anti-fascist composer for months because he is a brother of Gerhart Eisler, the House Committee on Un-American Activities has called on the Department of Justice to put the finishing touches to its persecution. The Justice Department, cooperating with a zeal which won the praise of Committee Chairman J. Parnell Thomas, has arrested Eisler and his wife for deportation proceedings. What a grotesque irony: Gerhart Eisler, who wants to go back to his homeland to take his place in the fight for a democratic Germany, is told he must go instead to an American jail. Hanns Eisler, who wants to remain in this country where his work has enriched our culture, is told he will be kicked back to Germany!

"It is time for all Americans who want to preserve the Bill of Rights, no matter what their political beliefs, to demand of Attorney General Tom Clark that he halt the persecution of Hanns Eisler. And let the protests resound also against the Un-American Committee's Hollywood inquisition which reopens in Washington October 20.

"We present Hanns Eisler's challenging statement to the Un-American Committee which he was not permitted to read at his hearing."

Eisler's interrogatory took place in Washington, D.C. from September 24–26, 1947. His statement was put on file, but he was not permitted to read it and his appeal was turned down.

1   The puppet cartoon film, *Pete Roleum and His Cousins* was an advertising film for the petroleum industry of the U.S.A. and was made for the World's Fair in New York in summer 1939. For the director, Joseph Losey, as well as

for the composer, Hanns Eisler, it meant the breakthrough into the film industry.

2 Some of the works mentioned by Eisler, which were performed in America had been composed earlier: *Divertimento für Bläserquintett*, 1923, *Kleine Sinfonie*, 1932, *Kammerkantaten für Gesang, zwei Klarinetten, Viola und Violoncello* and *Sonate für Violine und Klavier (Die Reisesonate)*, 1937.

Basic Social Questions
of Modern Music
1948

It is not possible to speak about the social basis of modern music without first trying to become clear about the difficulties and contradictions in music and musical life in general. For they are not only a characteristic feature of modern style, but they are also to be found in the very substance and history of bourgeois music, first in embryo, then in the process of growth and finally fully developed. Modern style therefore is only the result of a process that had already begun somewhere in the fifteenth and sixteenth centuries. The following comments are based on activities, experiences and observations made in America. They are therefore one-sided. But since music is vegetating under very particular social conditions in America, I hope this one-sidedness may be of some value. I must first say that I can only deal briefly with complicated phenomena, so that much can only be referred to or touched upon, though really requiring a lengthy and thorough explanation.

An American pupil of mine said to me once, "It doesn't matter whether my music is played or not, I am satisfied to put it down on paper. You never get an adequate interpretation nowadays, genuinely realizing the composer's intentions. Interpretation and realization deteriorate if an experienced and understanding audience doesn't exist. Genuine music can consequently only live as an idea and can no longer be conveyed or communicated to other people." It is not by chance that I heard this tragically eccentric but also pompously trivial assertion in Hollywood. It not only indicates futile work, disinclination, discontent and trouble in coming to terms with oneself and social conditions, but also indicates the most extreme contradiction, and that is the monopoly-capitalist culture-industry which is also now preparing to bring overheated eccentricity onto the market. (For the time being as accompaniment to a certain type of film or radio play.)

The cultural industry is certainly not disinclined and has no spiritual conflict. It is thoroughly optimistic, the optimism of a traveling salesman, who is sure that he will unload all his inferior wares on the gullible customers. The cultural industry loves people in its own way, as customers, or as the butcher loves his calf. In addition to producing its so-called entertainment music, it has also brought onto the market the works of the great masters in debased and incompetent arrangements. It has not only satisfied needs, it has created new ones. It has leveled out all distinctions, it has standardized and organized. It has intruded into all corners of art and has driven the artist to the wall. It has left its mark on the whole of musical life—in concerts the symphonies already sound like film music, and the serious composers are bought off by Hollywood, or write musicals. The artist himself is a lackey, an employee who can easily be dealt with. There is no question of discussion; if he opens his mouth, then out he goes! It is the cultural industry that has led to the boring uniformity in this profit-making economy. It has produced the filth, the inferiority, tediousness and emptiness of cultural life. It not only controls the mechanized means of producing music, such as film, radio, television and gramophone. It already controls concert life through the concert agencies, the book market through the book clubs and through the magazine supplements of the newspapers, in particular, the "comic strips"; it has become a partner in the newspaper monopolies and press agencies. Its profits are as immense as its power. It has turned genuine art into a commodity.

Of course, the cultural industry, like every other industry, satisfies needs. These needs arise from the necessity of the masses to reproduce the labor power that they have expended in alienated working processes. That is to say the needs arise from the necessity to have repose, to relax and to have amusement at any price and at a low one.

Of all the arts music is the most distant from the world of practical things and so it is most prone to be used as a sort of narcotic. It is said to arouse the emotions, though how this happens was never quite clear. In any case it appears to be the abstract opposite of emptiness and monotony in everyday life. The greater the emptiness and monotony, the sweeter the music.

The monopoly culture-industry is able to produce and distribute inferiority because of a kind of retarded development in listening. With some reservations we could say that listening has not been able to keep pace with the rapid development of technology and industry during the last 150 years. Whereas sight involves some exertion and action, listening still has something passive, placid and archaic about it. It has not been able, so to speak, to get used to the rational bourgeois world as a world of commodities. Taking in something merely by ear, compared with vision, still shows signs of pre-individualist, pre-capitalist community. Polyphonic style in particular points directly to this; it points to the past cult of the religious community, the community of the church. The inclusion and absorption of the individual in a community, the feeling of togetherness, of belonging, which all music arouses, must be considered music's most natural function. But even as its most natural function it is subject to the universal process of social development.

It is difficult to place the beginning of bourgeois music development in a definite political-historical period as is often done, for the development of music does not go parallel with socio-economic developments. It would be difficult to place the development of musical forms in direct relation to economic developments. Even where such a parallel seems to exist it is much more likely to be a multiple-mediated relation than a mechanically direct one.

The development of bourgeois music can most easily be understood as its emancipation from a religious cult function, its taking on a cultivating and civilizing function. Musically, this is displayed in the growth of homophonic style. The subjectivity of music is no longer directed at the dull church congregation, but at the cultivated listener. This emancipation towards a cultivating and civilizing character must be considered the real bourgeois feature in music. The emergence of the individual from the community did not go unpunished. It was certainly an historical necessity, but from the beginning, bourgeois music contained the canker that led to the disorders of modern style today, and which are only the extreme, final phase of a long process. There was and still is something in the nature of a bad conscience in homophonic music. From the musical-technical point of view, it is the simplicity, the naiveté of a highly developed homophonic style compared with polyphonic style. Subjectively, artistically, it appears as a vague feeling of being separated, of the insecurity of being isolated. The late periods of Mozart and Beethoven, with their desire for polyphonic, contrapuntal elements, could also perhaps be understood in this way. It is as if the bourgeois freed artist is not only uncertain in his actual way of life, but also in his artistic relation to the listener, looking back at the times when the ties between them were simpler and firm. But there is no going back. Nor is there in the history of art.

Although bourgeois society freed the musician from the servile conditions of the feudal period and the humiliations under which Haydn still had to live, at the same time it made him a sort of outlaw. It threw him onto the open market, exposed him to free competition, dependent on the caprices of the patrons, the publishers and the concert agencies. Sensitive artists were turned into bohemians and such artists as Schubert, Baudelaire and Hugo Wolf were tormented and ground down by poverty. It made life hell for the great masters and we must not be surprised if we hear this reflected in the music of the late bourgeois period. Something of it may be heard in the works of Beethoven, who was the greatest, yet the most sensitive. Beethoven not only expressed the rebellion and heroism of the revolutionary bourgeois individual, but also his despair, his isolation and depression. The intoxication of liberation was followed by disillusion; after the big bourgeois ideas came big business.

I will now leave the social basis of bourgeois music in general and speak in particular about the social basis of modern style. Here I must confine my subject to dealing with two schools, represented by Arnold Schönberg and Igor Stravinsky. This does not imply that I underestimate masters like Janáček, Bartók or Szymanovski; but Schönberg and Stravinsky have had the greatest influence on the music of today. Everyone has been influenced by them and everyone has learnt from them. Schönberg's twelve tone system on the one hand, and Stravinsky's neo-classicism on the other and the influence they exerted, represent the actual late bourgeois style. Schönberg's aesthetic ideas are fragmentary. They are to be found in his *Harmonielehre*[1] (Textbook of Harmony) and in his recently published collected lectures and essays. They are not of the same importance as his practical instructions and theories, for these have provided us with and taught us the greatest perception and deepest understanding of the great heritage of music from Bach to Brahms.

If Schönberg, for instance, states in his *Harmonielehre* that art must express truth, we must ask, "What truth?" Is it the knowledge of the social situation of music or is it only the development of musical material in the abstract? When Schönberg talks of artistic beauty, he means a new beauty in art which artists must honestly and genuinely aim at. Yet this new beauty in art appears in his works in the abstract, as a seeking after new nuances, new effects and sensations. It is reminiscent of expressionism before the First World War, and of the group round the *Blauer*

Reiter of Kandinsky, Kokoschka and Franz Marc. However, Schönberg's achievements are so extraordinary that we surely do not demand or expect music aesthetics from him.

Unfortunately, many of his adherents have done such private aestheticizing of their own and caused much mischief. Since Schönberg has written a great deal of vocal music, it is necessary to deal briefly with the subjects and the texts he chose. Besides the conventional lyrics, we find much that is whimsical and capricious. This is true in particular of the words to *Jakobsleiter*. It is all the sadder if you look at the brilliant sketches he made for it. Schönberg did not finish this work and, in my opinion, for good reasons. In his opera, *Von Heute auf Morgen*, text by Max Blonda[2], whom I have never heard of, the subject is the conjugal conflicts of well-dressed people. At the end a child—also well-dressed—asks, "Mummy, what are modern men?" The author, Mr. Max Blonda, naturally knows there's no such thing, man is man.

Well, without going into this petty-bourgeois attitude any further, we must admit from our knowledge of this music, that music is not music. Schönberg has composed a brilliant score of great mastery to this painfully unpleasant text, conceiving and depicting these well-dressed people as the future occupiers of air raid shelters, rather than habitués of night clubs. It is startling to see how this music illuminates the stupidity of the text, how it exposes the clichés and comments on the triviality of the conflict. This work is one of the most astonishing documents of modern music, with its extraordinary difficulties and complexities.

As a work of art *Pierrot Lunaire* is much more problematic. Against a background of wonderful chamber music poems by Albert Gireaud, feeble imitations of Verlaine, are declaimed by a narrator. To these poems, which with their naiveté could hardly be called works of art, Schönberg's music conforms and illustrates with feeling. The provincial demoniacal style of Gireaud together with exaggerated declamation, which Schönberg marked through the rhythm, is embarrassing and diverts from the music. I often suggested to Schönberg that he leave out the text, thus preserving the wonderful music as character pieces, but he would never hear of it.

The text to the opera *Die glückliche Hand* is by Schönberg himself and is equivalent to a drama by Kokoschka. *Die Erwartung* is a middling text by an excellent Viennese woman doctor. Yet to these operas with such questionable texts Schönberg wrote his best music.

Schönberg's nervousness, hysteria, panic and despair, loneliness and terror are expressed in the extreme. One could almost say that the characteristic feature of Schönberg's music is fear.

Long before aeroplanes were invented he anticipated the horrors of bombing attacks on people in air raid shelters. He is the lyric composer of the gas chambers of Auschwitz, of Dachau concentration camp, of the complete despair of the man in the street under the heel of fascism. That is his humanity. It is proof of Schönberg's genius and instinct that he gave expression to all these emotions at a time when the world seemed safe for the ordinary man in the street. Whatever one may say against him, he never lied.

Although Schönberg's historical achievement was audacious and new, he can be aped today by any mediocre music graduate of an average conservatory. Yet Schönberg's cloak of loneliness cannot be borrowed. Our times require and demand something new. Schönberg's school is closed and new pupils will fail.

In these works of Schönberg's middle period, which I consider to be his best, the prevalence of dissonances is no longer considered the characteristic feature. It is much more the disintegration of traditional diction–asymmetry, composing without musical themes, rapid contrasts and the variety of musical configurations. These works are practically unknown and their influence is small.

On the other hand, the twelve tone system, by means of which Schönberg tried to organize new musical material has made its way throughout the world. It has great dangers. Ideologically it has encouraged petty-bourgeois features among some composers, such as mysticism regarding numbers, astrology and anthroposophy. They can be found in the works of such prominent composers as Anton von Webern and Alban Berg. But it is not only the openly ideological aspect that is dangerous for imitators. The twelve tone technique is liable to become complicated in details, arising from the nature of the system. It makes it difficult for the composer and easy at the same time. In a bad twelve tone composition, what is correct only is the purely serial side, the arithmetical side. Musical logic, the development and continuation of musical ideas become mechanical, allowing everyone to make a fool of himself if he wants to. For nothing is simpler than to write down a twelve tone subject with its fundamental forms: inversion, cancrizans of the subject and cancrizans of the inversion. A copyist can easily transpose it to all intervals of the chromatic scale. The artistic material is thus pre-fashioned mechanically and undialectically. I always find it pathetic when a composer proudly explains that the bass is the cancrizans inversion of the upper voice. This pride is groundless in a style where complicated contrapuntal relations are pre-fashioned, in the same way as the keys are in a tonal composition. I should also have found it ridiculous if Czerny had proudly explained to me that his études are composed in C major. Especially the analyses of twelve tone compositions are full of such nonsense and are already being published today in books.

It would require the utmost mastery to compose a strong, precise, clear work under such preconditions which appears to be spontaneous and not a careful exercise. There is actually a contradiction between this new arrangement of material and the traditional musical forms, for instance, the sonata form. If we study Schönberg's wind quintet, the third and fourth string quartets, the violin concerto and the piano concerto, we can see not only how difficult Schönberg made it for himself, but also how difficult it indeed was for him. It is well-known that the sonata form developed in the period of tonality. The contrast between the first and second subjects is not only rhythmical and thematic, but in the first place also tonal. The main contrast between the exposition and the development lies in the tonal organization. The exact working out of the tonic key in the exposition corresponds with a looser manner, with a more driving character in the development. Without tonality the function of the recapitulation, namely to return to the original key, becomes an historical obligation and a hollow gesture, devoid of musical meaning. In the twelve tone system, because of the loss of tonality, the other elements of form must be specially exaggerated and developed. Transition passages, for example, can only work up thematic and rhythmical material, but cannot modulate, so that the second subject now arrived at, does not represent a new tonal field, but only a thematic and rhythmical one. Such contradictions between material and form prevent an exposition and development in twelve tone style from being essentially different, and have made the recapitulation grow from a varied repetition to a kind of third treatment of the thematic material. The spirit of the sonata is no longer present as a concrete form, but is only there in the abstract. It is a demolished house that is being offered as a home.

Now if such contradictions and difficulties occur in the works of a master as great as Schönberg, then you can easily imagine how hopeless the situation is for incompetent imitators. What may be regarded as problematic, yet interesting and stimulating as a music-historical phenomenon in the work of a master, is annoying, is great nonsense and sectarian snobbishness in his imitators. I recall with pleasure what Schönberg always said about such works, "I don't understand modern music at all, it is much too complicated and nervous. Why don't young composers write more simply?"

Imitation of music-historical phenomena not only annoys the ordinary listener, but is also objectionable to the expert, to whom it seems utter rubbish. Socially such works are more than isolated. Whereas bourgeois chamber music generally is of interest only to small circles of experts due to the decrease in home music-making, modern chamber music seems to be a sort of laboratory product for small performances of a laboratory character. I appreciate these concerts and music societies, since it is always useful for musicians, composers and instrumentalists to acquaint themselves with the most modern styles. Study and criticism, respect and doubt are necessary to counter boring, eclectic pedestrianism.

The second leading modern school is that of Stravinsky. But here I wish to limit myself to his neo-classical period, which has had the widest influence. Stravinsky's aesthetic theories—to be found in his autobiography[3]—are also fragmentary and are not his own. One need only look at Jean Cocteau's book *Le Coque et le harlequin* to know that they stem from him. If Schönberg is an isolated intellectual, Stravinsky is the "gentleman," completely at ease in the modern milieu. Stravinsky's neo-classical style is cautious, smart, cold, open, constructed and imitative. The main features of neo-classicism are impassiveness, the imperviousness of the artist to the object that he presents, coldness, a fixed manner of ornamentation, mechanical configuration, quotations from pre-Beethoven melismata, lack of motivation, the static, the non-symphonic, the shortness of forms. At the beginning neo-classicism outmoded the music of the nineteenth century. In the drawing rooms around 1923 it was fashionable to regard Beethoven as passé, pompous and over and done with.

Neo-classicism is a phenomenon of the big bourgeoisie. It has no relation, either spiritual or musical, to the great heritage of the revolutionary bourgeoisie. It is arrogant and cold to the man in the street; it is the musical style of "good society." Yet it would be wrong to disregard the progressive significance of many of Stravinsky's characteristics and methods and his incidental and ballet music in particular. Unfortunately, more of his weaknesses and bad habits are copied than his merits.

The weaknesses of neo-classicism are not only musical, but are openly ideological. It is the neo-Catholicism of Cocteau and Stravinsky which a number of considerable talents in Paris have turned to. Now neo-Catholicism must not be equated with simple religious needs, the belief in the moral heritage of Christianity. Neo-Catholicism flirts with the formal, the ceremonial, and cult in religion. It is more like religious formalism than belief. Neo-Catholicism has something mondaine, elegant and falsely modern about it. And that is why the Symphony of Psalms and Oedipus Rex by Stravinsky–the most important neo-classical works of our time–not only sound ceremonial and cult-like, but have a remarkable affinity to Wall Street, although it certainly has no cult significance.

In general, in its manner of expression neo-classicism deports itself like a member of good society, not too loud, not too soft, in a noncommittal way, trying to copy the inscrutable mask of a big banker, who in turn apes an actor trying to play the part of a financier. The German version of neo-classicism is *Spielfreudigkeit*. I have never clearly seen what this "joy in playing" means. Is the audience delighted that the cellist is playing, or is it the cellist who is delighted, because he is allowed to play? What is certainly clear about *Spielfreudigkeit* is the way of composing, avoiding anything expressive, showing preference for running configuration and simulating the skill of the old masters by a kind of dissonant, school-exercise counterpoint.

The only joyful thing about this "joy in playing" is the trick the composer is playing on us.

It is obvious that the art of "not expressing oneself" in neo-classicism is merely one particular form of expressing oneself, for even in the coldest music, the coldness is a form of expression. Both schools, Schönberg's expressionism and Stravinsky's neo-classicism seek in vain for firm ties. What the twelve tone system is to Schönberg, style imitation is to Stravinsky. The metaphysicism and numbers mysticism of Schönberg correspond to the formalism of Stravinsky's neo-Catholicism. So both schools seem identical, differing only in nuances. The security, the spiritual ties that Schönberg requires are pure craftsmanship and the working out of new musical material. The security that Stravinsky needs is imitation of style and the security of good society. Both masters are only able to hold their disintegrating material together by craftiness and artistic feats.

If I said earlier that the contradictions and difficulties of later bourgeois music are only the utmost form of a process, whose origins lie far back in the history of the bourgeoisie, one could glance at Hegel. In his lectures on aesthetics he said, "In modern time particularly, music, having drifted away from a clear content, has returned to its own element, but as a consequence, has lost even more power over the whole of man's inner self. For the pleasure it can offer can only touch one side of art—mere interest in the purely musical and skillful side of a composition. This side is a matter for experts and has little to do with general human interest in art."

The emancipation of music from the religious cult character to the cultivating, civilizing character has reached its final phase. After all the excesses and experiments, it appears today to be the job of music of our time to lead music back to a higher form of society, to lead it back from the private to the universal, perhaps at first in a somewhat more modest way. This higher form is a society of free men and women, where the exploitation of man by man has ended. Perhaps music will then take on a more friendly and more joyful character after this period of disinclination, trouble and self-torment.

In the remarkable book by the Chinese philosopher Me-Ti, (a contemporary of Confucius) *The Damnation of Music*, it says, "The practice of music has four disadvantages, the hungry are not fed, the cold are not clothed, the homeless are not sheltered and the desperate find no consolation." May the words of Me-Ti remind us as modern musicians who are fond of speculating, constructing and experimenting, that music is made by man for man.

Source: Hanns Eisler, *Reden und Aufsätze*, Winfried Höntsch, ed., Leipzig 1961, pp. 76–91.
EGW III/2 (in preparation).
Eisler delivered this lecture at the Second International Congress of Composers and Music Critics in Prague, May 1948. A stenciled copy of the translation handed out to the English-speaking participants at the congress was found among Eisler's posthumous papers. A new translation has been prepared for this edition from the stenciled copy from Prague.

1   At the time of Eisler's speech Arnold Schönberg's collected lectures and writings had not yet appeared. Apparently Eisler knew that an edition had been prepared and believed that it had already been published. However, it was first published under the title, *Style and Idea* in New York 1950.

2   It is odd that Eisler claims not to have known that Max Blonda, the author of the libretto of the opera *Von Heute auf Morgen*, was the pseudonym of Arnold Schönberg's wife, Gertrud.

3   Igor Stravinsky's autobiography appeared in Paris 1936, entitled, *Chroniques de ma vie*.

Thoughts on the Anniversary
of Beethoven's Death
1952

The greatness of Beethoven's music lies in the character of its expression: pathos without pompousness, heroism without bombast, feeling without sentimentality, compassion without self-indulgence, humor without archness, passion without hysteria.

He was accused of breaking all standards. He created his own standards and by these must he be measured.

When talking about Beethoven's *Volkstümlichkeit*[1], one should say that he is the criterion of it. For in addition to his very popular symphonies and overtures he wrote complicated chamber music. His last string quartets and piano sonatas, his variations (the Eroica and Diabelli Variations) and finally the great String Quartet-fugue in B flat major have not yet become universally accepted. But an understanding of these works is a measure of genuine music culture.

With regard to Beethoven's counterpoint exercises, which he did for his teachers Haydn and Albrechtsberger, nothing came to him easily. Can it be said that the young lion was feeling his way clumsily? No, one can hardly detect anything of the young lion here. But the diligence with which Beethoven endeavored first of all to acquire a traditional technique is still an example for us today.

As to his sketchbooks: fantasy and construction are interwoven. Fantasy stimulates his construction and construction stimulates fantasy. Spontaneity and the artist's intellect are not antagonistic.

He was not one of those lackadaisical music-makers. He planned and built his works conscientiously. The music-maker in him enlivened the material.

In the big forms he scrupulously works out the tiniest details. He is no "al fresco" musician.

One could characterize Beethoven's music as courageous music. The characteristic of courage to fight is to be found in almost all of his works.

The plebeian and the tribune of the people was contemptuous of renegades.

On the origin of *Fidelio*: a French composer[2] had his revolutionary opera *Leonore* produced in Vienna. Beethoven congratulated him saying, "I thought your opera was excellent. I shall compose it."

Concerning the Ninth Symphony: long passages of the work express mourning, despair and loneliness. The scherzo[3] is thoroughly novel in its desperate gaiety, followed by the great and heroic finale. This is no cheap heroism. In content and form this symphony was absolutely unprecedented so that narrow-minded people like the composer Spohr[4] were still condemning it in the middle of the 19th century as muddled, incomprehensible and hardly playable.

The Piano Sonata opus 27, "quasi una fantasia," is unfortunately called the "Moonlight Sonata."[5] To me, this decorative title is nonsense, and misleading. This sonata has nothing to do with moonlight.

Shrewd American entrepreneurs, in their radio advertisements, utilize an arrangement of this sonata for choir and orchestra: Beethoven's lightly indicated melody in the piano triplets is played by the strings unctuously and overloaded with expression. Against this a choir sings a schmaltzy chorale to the moon.

This is pure barbarism and it should be said here and now, especially since friends have told me that a Beethoven symphony was performed in Weimar by an orchestra of accordions.

Source: Typescript, Hanns Eisler Archives.
The article appeared in the weekly *Sonntag*, Berlin, March 23, 1952 under the title, *Zu Beethoven's Todestag*. EGW III/2 (in preparation).

1 *Volkstümlichkeit* (literally: popularity), an expression considered by Eisler to be over-used, was meant to describe a certain quality of art, i.e. readily accepted by the people.

2 J. N. Bouilly's *Léonore ou l'amour conjugal*, the idea for Beethoven's *Fidelio*, had already been composed in 1798 in Paris by Pierre Gaveaux (1761–1825).

3 In the Ninth Symphony the movement with scherzo character, but not marked as a scherzo, takes the place of the second movement, innovative at that time.

4 Louis Spohr (1784–1859), in his time a well-known composer, violin virtuoso and conductor, recalls in his autobiography (published in 1860) his meetings with Beethoven and the impression he made with his music. He believed that in the works following the Seventh Symphony "a falling-off of Beethoven's creative powers" could be observed. Due to his deafness it had not been possible to prevent his drive for originality from going astray. His

works had become "more and more baroque, more confused and incomprehensible. Yes, I must even count the esteemed Ninth Symphony among such works. The first three movements, despite individual flashes of genius, appear to me to be worse than all the eight earlier symphonies taken together; while the fourth movement is so monstrous, so without taste and so trivial in its conception of Schiller's Ode, that I still cannot understand how a genius like Beethoven could have written it down. For me this is fresh proof of what I said in Vienna, that Beethoven lacked aesthetic refinement and a feeling for beauty."

5 The name "Moonlight Sonata" for Beethoven's Piano Sonata in C sharp minor, op. 27, No. 2 was coined by the Berlin music critic and writer Ludwig Rellstab (1799 to 1860) about 1850. He said that the first movement with its melody floating over the dark minor triplets reminded him of a moonlight night on the Lake Lucerne.

Bertolt Brecht and Music
1957

"Noteworthy are not only the serious acts of great and noble men: I believe that what they do in hours of recreation and play is also worthy of attention."

Xenophon, "The Feast of Kallias"

1. The Baden Didactic Play
In 1929 Brecht wrote a didactic play for the music festival in Baden-Baden. The music was written by Paul Hindemith. It was a great production and wonderful music.

One episode was a clowning scene: after some instructive discussion on the weakness of human nature, two clowns saw off the feet of a third clown. These feet were stilts crudely made of wood. This rough joke appalled many spectators. Some fainted, although only wood was being sawed, and the performance was certainly not naturalistic. I sat next to a well-known music critic who fainted. I helped him out and got him a glass of water.

When I told Brecht this, he said: "That's really silly, the man wouldn't faint in a symphony concert, though they are always sawing there—on the violins. (Brecht hated violins.) I am disappointed."

2. Brecht and Arnold Schönberg
With some hesitation I introduced Brecht to my teacher Arnold Schönberg. It was in 1942 in Hollywood. There were two reasons for me to hesitate: I did not want my respected and ailing teacher Arnold Schönberg to be upset by some remark of Brecht's which Brecht could not anticipate; and also did not want Arnold Schönberg to make one of his stupid remarks against socialism, which I was used to

172

taking in silence, since he was sick and must not be excited. However I could not demand this of Brecht, for Brecht was in this respect loud, sharp and uncompromising; and I did not want Brecht to be loud, sharp and uncompromising to the sick man Schönberg.

Things went better than I expected, though Schönberg had no idea who Brecht was, and Brecht rejected Schönberg's music in a manner which a modern composer will think monstrous: "Schönberg is too melodious for me, too sweet." After an hour's exchange of politenesses, Schönberg related one of his experiences with donkeys. Brecht was delighted, the two had found common ground, Brecht too had experiences with donkeys.

Schönberg related: "Once I climbed a hill, and since I have a weak heart the steep path was very difficult for me. But in front of me there walked a donkey. He did not walk up the steep path, but always in zigzag left and right of the path, thus compensating for the steepness. So I imitated him, and now I can say that I have learned something from a donkey." Brecht made from this a poem in honor of Arnold Schönberg's seventieth birthday. It will be found among Brecht's papers.

3. Misuc

Brecht's rejection of certain sorts of music was so extreme that he invented another variety of music-making, which he called "misuc." Misuc he regarded as a way of music-making basically differing from music, since it is misuc and not music.

Brecht's efforts in this field were really based upon his dislike of Beethoven's symphonies (though he loved the music of Bach and Mozart). For thirty years I tried to prove to him that Beethoven was a great master. He often admitted as much to me; but after doing so he was ill-tempered and looked at me distrustfully. "His music always reminds one of paintings of battles," he said. By this Brecht meant that Beethoven had fought Napoleon's battles once again on music paper. And since he did not admire the originals–Brecht had not much symphathy for battles–he did not like the imitations either. For this reason, and for other reasons too, he invented what he called misuc.

For a musician it is difficult to describe misuc. Above all it is not decadent and formalist, but extremely close to the people. It recalls, perhaps, the singing of working women in a back courtyard on Sunday afternoons. Brecht's dislike of music ceremoniously produced in large concert halls by painstaking gentlemen in tails also forms a constituent of misuc. In misuc nobody may wear tails and nothing may be ceremonious. I hope I am interpreting Brecht correctly when I add that misuc aims at being a branch of the arts which avoids something frequently produced by symphony concerts and operas–emotional confusion. Brecht was never ready to hand in his brain at the cloakroom. He regarded the use of reason as one of the best recreations.

Brecht's strivings for reason in music are a heavy blow for us musicians. For in the case of music, where is reason? I have friends who would not go through fire in the cause of reason in music.

Writing these lines, I recall that Brecht accused me of having a skeptical and condescending attitude towards misuc, his invention. Unfortunately he was right.

Source: *Bertolt Brecht und die Musik* in *Sinn und Form*, special issue on Bertolt Brecht, Berlin 1957, Nos. 1–3, pp. 439–41. This translation is by John Peet and taken from *Brecht As They Knew Him*, ed. Hubert Witt, Seven Seas Books, Berlin, 1974.
EGW III/2 (in preparation).

On Good Listening
1957

We must get away from a certain conventionality in our concert programs. For example, to my knowledge there are new vocal works (music for voice) in both big and small forms and with a socialist content which are hardly ever or never performed in our regular symphony concerts, although the Union of Composers and the Music Department of the Ministry of Culture make great efforts to promote such works. The proposed conference on culture could help the composers on this question and thus contribute to acquainting our public with a new kind of concert. I consider instruction in the arts in schools of particular importance. A lot has to be improved here. As to music lessons, they can also be made amusing and interesting for children by utilizing their instinct for play. Abundant possibilities exist for training boys and girls in listening. There can be no musical culture without good listening and without aural training. And indeed, these young people will be the public in our concert halls and opera houses in future.

To put it bluntly: first, we must surmount a generally conspicuous musical illiteracy. By this I mean that despite our great musical traditions there is a specific lack of basic musical knowledge, due to the fatal heritage of class privilege in the musical life of capitalist society. Admittedly our great classical composers, such as Bach and Beethoven make very high demands of the listeners.

Take for instance, the following program—Johann Sebastian Bach: the Chromatic Fantasy and Fugue; Ludwig van Beethoven: the Hammerklavier Sonata and the Diabelli Variations.

In my opinion a program like this assumes that the listener is already used to extremely complicated and differentiated music. Yet precisely this exacting program is played frequently in concert halls in Moscow by the famous pianist Svyatoslav Richter to audiences of two thousand people. I do not know whether we could expect the same measure of success today in our capital.

Nevertheless, the aim of cultivating our popular music is not just to guide people to an understanding of simple pieces which can straightaway be sung or whistled, but to open up to them the great treasure house of our classical German music. Now it would be foolish to overwhelm a fifty-year-old activist steelworker for whom Paul Lincke's compositions mean amusement and relaxation, with the most difficult classical works—there are lighter ones. Still, in our workers' and peasants' state we have every possibility of educating the grandchild of this worker to become a connoisseur of music.

For that very reason it seems to me that the intensification of music instruction in schools and the training of music teachers, are the fundamental tasks in building a socialist music culture. Naturally, I expect the cultural conference to invite and especially to stimulate musicians to write new musical works, expressing more forcibly the socialist content of our lives. I am not only thinking of mass songs and choral pieces, or other simple forms. Music has so many genres. In every one of them you can find some way of expressing what is new and also useful to us, provided that you are sufficiently courageous and inventive. We need new ideas.

So I think that at the cultural conference special stress should be laid on discussing new ways and means of bringing composers and the broad public closer together. And it is important after that to draw the practical conclusions from all the manifold suggestions made. Then our concert halls will be fuller.

Source: *Zum guten Hören* in *BZ am Abend,* Berlin, August 15, 1957.

In preparation for a Conference on Culture organized by the Socialist Unity Party of Germany on October 23–24, 1957, the public was called upon to discuss ideas and proposals on topical questions of cultural policy. At the request of the widely read Berlin evening paper Hanns Eisler wrote about what he considered the most important problems.

Song Born of Struggle
Interview with Hanns Eisler
1957

Professor Eisler, you were kind enough to agree to say something today about traditions in proletarian music.

First, I would like to point out that these traditions in general are little known. The traditions in proletarian music, perhaps it would be better to say the workers' music movement, go back a long way. I don't want to give a lengthy historical discourse here, but would like to point out that by the middle of the nineteenth century, workers' choir music already existed.

At that time it was closely connected with the Social-Democratic working-class movement?

With the young socialist working-class movement. It was certainly still unsophisticated. It had all the elements, not always the best, of the folk song tradition and the journeyman's songs. Though at that time typical workers' songs were springing up which today are a part of the heritage of the workers. For example, in Leipzig in 1860 workers' songs were sung, and they were distinctly different from those of the bourgeois *Liedertafel* literature (glees).

Where did these workers' choral societies find their texts? Were they simple folk song texts or were they used for political agitation at that time?

They were the generally known folk song melodies, not always very well arranged. The middle of the nineteenth century produced many great revolutionary poets, Herwegh, for example, whose brilliant poem *Bet und arbeit, ruft die Welt*[1] (Prayer and Labor Calls the World) became the hymn of the young socialist working-class movement. Composers came from the ranks of the workers' choir conductors; they were either choir members themselves or teachers, for instance, the popular Uthmann[2], a workers' choir conductor and composer, whose active period was roughly between 1890 and 1910. One of the favorite choral pieces was, *Die Fahn soll stehen, wenn der Mann auch fällt* (The flag shall fly, though the man may fall).

That concerns workers' songs and vocal music. Was there also a tradition in workers' instrumental music?

Of course. There were workers' orchestras very early on, which, depending on the region, were similar to good or bad amateur orchestras. They naturally specialized in such famous workers' songs as the *Internationale* and the *Marseillaise*. In the Weimar Republic one often heard Russian revolutionary marches, melodies which were played quite proficiently and which always made a deep impression on our audience. No matter what the performance was like, this music could only be heard at workers' gatherings, and let no snob, no bourgeois snob, have the audacity to judge it other than with respect.

You have just mentioned the twenties. Wasn't it at this time that the workers' music movement reached its climax?

It reached its climax, because many experts including musicians, poets and artists of all kinds collaborated. Imagine, for example, there was one production in 1928–29 which included the work of the poets Bertolt Brecht, Erich Weinert and my friend Becher, actors and singers such as Ernst Busch, Helene Weigel and composers—pardon me—like myself, but also my friend Ernst Hermann Meyer and others. So you can see that artists who play an international role today, were at that time already closely associated with the working-class movement. These productions were of a very high standard. They were modern in the best sense of the word, also artistically modern.

When in the twenties did these performances with workers' songs first take place? When did Ernst Busch make his first appearance?

Ernst Busch first appeared together with me in 1928, and that was at a workers' gathering where the Soviet poet Mayakovsky was also on the program. I must say it was such an astounding success that Ernst Busch became a household name overnight for the Berlin working class.

What did he sing at that time?

Songs to texts by Brecht, Erich Weinert and Tucholsky. It led to close cooperation with Brecht, who took a great interest in Ernst Busch as singer and actor. But Brecht also wrote some songs together with me for Helene Weigel; one was *Wiegenlieder für Arbeitermütter* (The Cradle Songs for Working-Class Mothers). Then Brecht and I worked together on the drama *Die Mutter* (The Mother) and on the didactic play *Die Maßnahme* (The Measures Taken).

Where were these proletarian mass songs performed which were written at that time?

No bar was too small for Ernst Busch, Helene Weigel, Brecht and me to perform in, and there was no hall too big, no theater too elegant for us to perform in either. The première of *Die Massnahme* took place in the old Philharmonic Hall in Bernburger Strasse. Yet the next evening Ernst Busch sang, with me at the piano, in a tiny bar near Alexanderplatz with just as much pleasure.

In this way you, Ernst Busch and Bertolt Brecht played a direct part in the political struggles of the day!

Yes. We certainly did! If anything new occurred, the first one to telephone me was Brecht, "We really must do something about that rightaway."

Could you give us a concrete example?

Well, Brecht wrote ballads about the notorious Paragraph 218[3] and also about the *Osthilfe*[4] scandal. We wrote the *Arbeitslosenlied* (Song of the Unemployed) during the time of great unemployment. The election campaign of 1929 was a topic for us. During this campaign the Social-Democratic leadership in Berlin distributed pieces of soap which had *Vote SPD* on the paper wrapping. To see that, make up a song and compose it, was a natural for our group. It was the *Seifenlied*[5] (Soap Song). Now I don't want to offend any Social-Democratic friends—but the line of our refrain ran, "We'll wash our hands clean again." Ernst Busch sang this marvelously and the audience was greatly amused. An intelligent Social-Democratic comrade probably would have laughed as much as a Communist comrade or a non-party person. It was what you might call "hot." And it was the necessary spice in this election campaign. I recall with pleasure the laughter which went up when Ernst Busch simply announced the *Seifenlied* with his knowing smile. The applause lasted two minutes before he could start singing.

These traditions of workers' music were of course interrupted in 1933. How were they carried on in emigration?

We continued them in the same way as in Germany, only under more difficult circumstances. New languages had first to be learned. We were also hampered as political emigrants. All the same we did what we could.

What songs did you write during this time?

The *Einheitsfrontlied*[6] (United Front Song) to name just one. It was written in London in 1934, because after the Peoples' Front Congress the question of the unity of the working people was urgent.

Brecht rang me up and said that we ought to write a song about it. The next day Ernst Busch sang it in English.

And a few weeks later it was being sung by the workers of many countries, wasn't it?

Yes, indeed.

You mention Brecht frequently, and his participation in the political day-to-day struggles of the time.

It is really not known enough. When it was necessary Brecht wrote cabaret sketches for the Berlin workers and that was right. He did it brilliantly, which we should not forget.

These traditions going back to the middle of the last century and reaching their climax in the twenties, were taken up again in our Republic after 1945, weren't they?

Yes, that's true, we can learn from these traditions. For instance, flexibility in our means, versatility in our methods, vigilance in our political everyday life. All this stimulates certain genres of music. As musicians we should remember that today. Unquestionably it is a tradition which we urgently ought to continue. Only recently I was at Werner Seelenbinder Hall for a dress rehearsal, the one before the performance, of the 40th anniversary celebration of the October Revolution. Here my friend, Kuba[7], came along and handed me a little poem. Could you do that quickly, he asked. It would be fine if we could include it in the program. So right then and there I composed it and rehearsed it with Gisela May.[8]

Was that the Sputnik Song?

No. The Sputnik Song was later. This was Two Sisters, Moscow and Berlin. But just before the performance an excited young man came running up to us backstage with another five verses saying wouldn't we like to add them as well. So we quickly went through them right before going on and sang the new song. It was early on a Sunday that the Sputnik was first known about and in the evening we sang a new song about it at a mass meeting in front of seven thousand people. I hadn't experienced such joy in Berlin for a long time: the artist's joy in the doing without any fuss. Gisela May was an enormous success which she well deserved.

Does this carrying on of tradition only apply to workers' songs, or does it also apply to instrumental music, to opera and other genres of music?

It does. We also used to write works for orchestras, oratorios, chamber music and cantatas. Today, where we have the power, a composer should be master of all forms. I must say, self-critically if you like, that we haven't accomplished enough by a long way. If only we would try to use our everyday life as a starting point, then we would see how quickly our new public would react. It shouldn't of course be one-sided. Our composers can work in peace and quiet at a symphony that perhaps has no direct connection with everyday life, but which is related to it in another way. The one thing does not exclude the other. It doesn't mean that now every musician must write a topical song for cabaret. But he shouldn't act in a superior way nor turn inward. If you like, "Go off for three months and write a symphony, but come back with your symphony and then compose something else." Work is many-sided and there is a wealth of possibilities for us!

Source: *Das Lied, im Kampfe geboren* in Hanns Eisler, *Reden und Aufsätze*, W. Höntsch, ed. Leipzig 1961, pp. 127–33. EGW III/8 (in preparation).
This interview given in December 1957 was broadcast in the series *Ereignisse und Erscheinungen* (Events and Facts). Eisler made some minor alterations to the publication.

1 *Bet und arbeit* (Prayer and Labor), the poem by Georg Herwegh (1817–1875), was written in 1864 on the suggestion of Ferdinand Lassalle (1825–1864), the founder and president of the *Allgemeine Deutsche Arbeiterverein* (General German Working Men's Association), as the association's hymn. The composition for four-part male choir by the famous conductor and composer Hans von Bülow under the pseudonym of Solinger, proved to be too complicated and did not become popular. The text has frequently been composed since, but never with any resounding success.

2 Gustav Adolf Uthmann (1867–1920), a dyer by trade, became later the manager of a medical insurance society in Barmen. Musically self-taught, he conducted the Barmen Workers' Choral Society and composed about 400 choral pieces.

3 Paragraph 218, anti-abortion paragraph of the German Penal Code of the Weimar Republic.

4 *Osthilfe,* literally "Eastern Aid." Government aid program for farmers in Eastern Germany initiated in 1930. The aid mainly went to the Junkers. In 1932 it was revealed that President Hindenburg had received large sums.

5   The *Seifenlied* (Soap Song) was composed by the cabaret conductor Otto Stransky (1869–1932), the text was
written by Julian Arendt. Both belonged to a group of
progressive artists around Hanns Eisler und Ernst Busch.

6   The *Einheitsfrontlied* (United Front Song) became
known internationally largely through the First International Workers' Music Olympiad in Strasbourg, June 8–10,
1935. It was sung by Ernst Busch, accompanied by Hanns
Eisler, together with 3,000 working-class singers and the
audience joining in. Eisler made an error in the date when
historically placing the *Einheitsfrontlied.* He said that the
date of the composition was 1936 (corrected in this book)
and mentioned it in connection with the Seventh Congress
of the Communist International, held in 1935 in Moscow
and which initiated the *Volksfrontbewegung* (The Popular
Front Movement). One can see how this happened for the
song helped to strengthen the fight for the anti-fascist
united front. The suggestion for the creation of such a
song, by the way, was made by the International Revolutionary Theater League in Moscow, whose chairman Erwin
Piscator wrote to Brecht saying that, if possible, he should
write "a good united front song" together with Eisler.

7   Kuba (Kurt Bartel, 1914–1967) poet and dramatist,
wrote the texts to *Zwei liebevolle Schwestern* (Two Loving
Sisters) and *Sputnik,* referred to by Eisler.

8   Gisela May, actress at the Berliner Ensemble and
chanson singer, a prominent Eisler interpreter in the
G.D.R.; has popularized Eisler's songs on concert tours in
many countries, including the U.S.A.

I Once Knew a Headwaiter

I once knew a headwaiter who gave me a very good critical assessment of the behavior of conductors. He was a music-lover and by chance I sat next to him at a concert. First of all he criticized the professional attire of the conductor, namely his dress suit. It is not by chance that the headwaiter and the conductor wear the same sort of apparel when carrying out their occupation. The conductor apparently also has something to serve. Well, on the question of serving the headwaiter was an expert, far superior to the conductor as to tact, taste and refinement. He said to me, "If I were to serve my dishes with such a display of grimaces, bombastic and saccharine gestures, I wouldn't last eight days. It is quite impossible when the conductor starts putting on a sweet expression before a melodious theme begins. He really can't predigest the music. After all, I cannot place a piece of meat on the table before a guest while I chew and belch. My deportment as a waiter," he said, "must be unprejudiced by the kind of meals served. I must serve politely and with facility, but I cannot fit my way of serving to the dishes. I would not place a beef-steak on the table with a solemn gesture or stewed fruit with a delicate mien. There are such idiots to be found among waiters, but they don't last long."

A vocal concert is also extraordinary. A lady in evening clothes holding a bouquet of flowers appears on the stage. A gentleman in evening dress is sitting at the piano, this time not a headwaiter, but merely a waiter at table. The lady sings songs: *Ich grolle nicht*[1] (I shall not mourn), *Wie bist Du, meine Königin* (What art thou like, my queen),

186

and similar stuff from the nineteenth century. I consider this kind of recital stupid and absurd. Music is a social art to the highest degree and the social forms of interpretation cannot be taken over willy-nilly. Schubert's songs were composed for a small circle and especially for playing at home. This kind of interpretation distorts them.

Source: Typescript, Hanns Eisler Archives.
EGW III/2 (in preparation).

1 The song *Ich grolle nicht* from the song cycle, *Dichter-liebe* by Robert Schumann, words by Heinrich Heine. *Wie bist du, meine Königin,* song by Johannes Brahms.

On Stupidity in Music
Imaginary Dialogue
1958

First Series

How does stupidity show itself in music?

Stupidity in music can be expressed in tones—sequences of
tones can be called stupid. But also general human stupidity can be widespread in music. In vocal works it is the
relation of the music to the text. An example: a composer
set to music Goethe's poem, *Ich ging im Walde so für mich
hin* (I was wandering in the forest, by myself). He did it
polyphonically, like a motet. He had not understood that
Goethe's popularly written lyric was progressive in its
subjectivity. It was no longer a bucolic poem, nor a court
love poem, but here Goethe expressed his subjective emotions and to go back to the baroque method of composing
I consider stupid. Such poems should not be composed
today. There are enough wonderful musical settings by
Schubert, Schumann and minor masters. But certain composers try to find abstract, collective emotion in the baroque period, which they profess to feel, or as they vaguely
call it "common experience." And here it must be stated once
and for all that there is nothing more boring or dumb than
second or third rate baroque music. Baroque style today is
escape into music history. Composers in this style believe
they have thus overcome the refined and certainly overheated
subjectivity of the old avant-garde and have acquired
social conscience. That, I deem to be stupid, because they are
trying to clothe reality in baroque sequences, but reality is
much more complicated and thus cannot be so disguised.

You consider both stupid: the general attitude of the composer and the actual method of composition?

Yes, they produce each other, without question.

Would you also consider the so-called Spielmusik *movement stupid?*

Yes, when you hear talk of the "community-building" spirit through the "joy in playing" then I become suspicious and immediately wonder what sort of community is going to be built and why these pieces of music, mostly pseudo-baroque, should arouse the joy in playing. It is bad music.

Isn't bad music always stupid?

No. Bad music may be degenerate, but in order to endure it must possess a quality of vulgar sensuality.

Do you include so-called trivial dance and entertainment music among bad music?

Yes. It is all the more dangerous, the more it is commercialized.

And don't you consider that stupid?

Dangerous things are unfortunately mostly not stupid. By the way, I now want to contradict myself and give you something to think about, which I would like to call "in praise of bad music." The following sentences can be found in *Les plaisirs et les jours,* the youthful work of the French writer Marcel Proust: "Pour out your curses on bad music, but not your contempt! The more bad music is played or sung (and usually more passionately than good music) the more it is filled with tears, with human tears. It has a place low down in the history of art, but high up in the history of the emotions of the human community. Respect (I do not say love) for ill music is not in itself a form of charity, it is much more the awareness of the social role of music. The people always have the same messengers and bearers of bad tidings in times of calamity and radiant happiness—bad musicians. Here, the horrible refrain, rejected at first hearing by every sensitive and well-trained ear, preserves the secret of numberless personal life stories, to whom it meant fertile inspiration and ever-ready consolation. A book of poor melodies, dog-eared from much use, should touch us like a town or a tomb. What does it matter that the houses have no style, or that the gravestones disappear beneath stupid inscriptions or banal ornamentation."

When did Proust write that?

In the last years of the nineteenth century. The young Proust did not yet know the dreadful flowering of commercial entertainment music.

Can we liquidate bad music and if so when?

When the peoples no longer need these messengers and bearers of bad tidings. That is to say with the blossoming of socialism and Communism, where the actual basis of bad music will have been done away with, that is, musical illiteracy which is brought about by social conditions.

Shouldn't the fight against musical illiteracy be combined with the struggle against decadence?

As a Marxist I think a difference must be made between two forms of decadence, one alien to the people and one close to them. Some of my friends believe that decadence alien to the people is the more dangerous. I consider decadence close to the people to be the most dangerous. This kind of decadent music—commercial jazz and plagiarized entertainment music is the daily method of blunting the ears and the sensibilities of the listeners. From early morning till late at night it is spread by way of the mechanized means of reproduction. It expresses a mendacious optimism that is absolutely unjustified, a flat pseudo-humanity, something like "Aren't we all?," a stuffy petty-bourgeois eroticism to put you off. Feeling is replaced by sentimentality, strength by bombast, humor by what I would call silliness. It is stupid to the highest degree.

And decadence alien to the people?

It is often difficult to discuss it. Once, while sitting in a restaurant here, one of my friends was telling me how he hated and how disgusted he was by the decadence of Arnold Schönberg, of Kafka and also despite everything, of Picasso. He had to speak very loudly since the café orchestra was playing a potpourri of some nonsensical operetta. As he had to raise his voice more and more, he got more and more excited. Just as he was disgustedly pointing out the lack of melody in Schönberg and certain pornographic traits in Proust's novel *A la recherche du temps perdu*, the orchestra blared out the waltz *Küssen ist keine Sünd*[1] (Kissing is no sin). But it was hardly possible to understand anything above the din of the bad music. So we were silent.

Isn't there also stupidity in concert music and opera?

An enormous amount. Especially among the Wagnerians. Think of the extent of the stupidity in a work as popular as *Rosenkavalier*. Apology for the peasant-exploiter Ochs von Lerchenau through comedy, the run-down bourgeoisie enjoying their humiliation on the opera stage, this Viennese version of Bismarck's conception of mixing the plutocracy with the Junkers. In *Die Meistersinger* Wagner has a bit more bourgeois dignity, although there too, the wealthy merchant's daughter marries the Junker. Still, his Hans Sachs is a man for all that. This hearty, self-confident petty bourgeois sees everything happening in the world as folly. That is monetheless stupidity—with class. But when you see how, with such a pastmaster as Richard Strauss, vulgar stupidity takes triumphant possession of our opera stages, wreaking permanent havoc, then you can just imagine what the plagiarists are going to offer us. Ever since my youth I have been having arguments with my conductor friends over the tin-plated humor and nauseous saccharinity of the *Rosenkavalier* score. And in addition, this atrocious Wagnerian illustrative technique! If a dog is mentioned, then the orchestra barks, if a bird is mentioned then the orchestra cheeps, if death is mentioned then the gentlemen of the trombones have to exert themselves, if it is love then there are the divided high violins in E major, and at the triumph the trusty percussion also joins in. It is unbearable!

Isn't that being too one-sided and exaggerated? Aren't you forgetting the beauties of the score because of some inaptitudes?

When stupidity is also beautiful, then I think of *The Damnation of Music* by Me-Ti 600 years B.C. "If the nobles of the country really have the welfare of the people at heart, they should prevent and forbid music wherever it makes an appearance. For the fact that the people practise music has four disadvantages. The hungry are not fed, the cold are not clothed, the homeless are not sheltered and . . ." the desperate find consolation. Me-Ti put it differently, he meant that the desperate did not find consolation. I would like to change this sentence. If I think of the stupidity in music I am of the opinion that the desperate do find consolation.

Your quotation from Me-Ti was not quite understood by some of my friends. Whom do you actually mean when you say, "The desperate find consolation?"

The desperate!

But isn't consolation the real aim of art, especially of music?

Concerning consolation, I can tell you something from the secret documents of the Austro-Hungarian state police in the year 1805 in Vienna, which says: "In times like the present, where manifold sufferings affect the character of the people, the police must pay more regard than ever to the distractions of the people. The most dangerous hours are in the evening. How can these hours be better and more harmlessly spent than by listening to music?"

But Eisler, 1805 was the year Beethoven composed his third symphony,[2] the "Eroica." Did the police chiefs want the Viennese to listen to this revolutionary music?

You overestimate the intelligence of the state police in 1805. Music was music, something for distraction. And now since our dialogue is proceeding by leaps and bounds, making no claim to be systematic or to provide axioms, I will jump over one hundred and fifty years and let you consider the following. "There are perhaps three such measures: powerful deflections, which cause us to make light of our misery; substitutive satisfactions, which diminish it; and intoxicating substances, which make us insensitive to it . . . The substitutive satisfactions, as offered by art, are illusions. They are responsible, in certain circumstances, for the useless waste of a large quota of energy which might have been employed for the improvement of the human lot."

That could mean stupidity in music too borders on the criminal. Who wrote it?

Sigmund Freud in 1927 and the booklet is entitled, *Das Unbehagen in der Kultur*[3] (Civilization and Its Discontents).

But, Eisler, you are making a jump from The Damnation of Music *of Me-Ti from 600 B.C. to Sigmund Freud in 1927.*

This jump is necessary in order to describe stupidity in music. I have to go a long way backwards to take a long run in order to jump.

As far as jumping is concerned, don't jump too far—think of the Wagnerians. Are there still such people who warrant your exasperation?

Yes, in some towns of our good Germany we have *Besitzer kleiner Wagnereien.** They are small traders who haven't got much to offer compared with the modern department stores, but since they no longer play a role, they play a role, that of the backward spheres. That shouldn't be underestimated. In the same way as the small traders are faced with the department store, or in socialism as the small retailer is faced with the state trading organization, these businesses are faced with the modern music industry.

Can the development of the so-called modern music industry be compared with handicrafts and small merchants?

Undoubtedly. Some time or other someone must make clear that the punctualistic, serial music, *musique concrète*, electronic music and so on represent the real triumph of pedestrian handicraft with one restriction. Handicraft for

---

* Eisler uses a pun. *Besitzer kleiner Wagnereien* (small wheelwrights) which alludes to Richard Wagner.

all its stupid and dull routine is based on a certain ability. But in these modern styles often not even the routine of handicraft is achieved.

By that you mean that modern handicraft is not only stupid, but cannot even produce stupidity properly?

True, to illustrate, let us first take the stupidity of the twelve tone system. If in a composition stupidity is established as the basic form of a twelve tone subject, then there is a) stupidity in the shape of the basic form, b) stupidity inverted, so it remains stupid, c) the cancrizans form, still stupid and d) the inversion of the cancrizans form, stupid.

Eisler, now I have caught you. Didn't you have twelve tone pieces published in 1924 and even up to the present you have continued to use this technique of composing, often to the consternation of your friends. And now you are against it. Have you turned your back on it?

No. But the pre-fashioning of the material of the twelve tone system offers enormous possibilities to stupidity, which I also deplore. It makes it possible for anyone of average intelligence to change into a blockhead quickly, and for small primitive talents to drape themselves with scholarship.

Then you are for and against?

Exactly. The use of the twelve tone method should at least depend on the genre. A children's song is not a string quartet, a symphonic movement not a workers' song. Anyone who muddles up the genres will remain a fool. Of course, a fool on his own hook!

How can this criticism be reconciled with modern music theory?

The music theory of our time should be based only on dialectical materialism. But that has not even been touched on. The whining of the disappointed petty bourgeois and of the offended salaried employee can also be found in music. It seems to be one of the chief features of music under capitalist conditions. There are music theoreticians in West Germany—the most gifted—who accuse today's modern music of commercializing Schönberg's fear, panic, hysteria and loneliness. The fundamental characteristics of Schönberg and his school are already being sold like coca-cola. In the attempt to technicalize music, like *musique concrète*, electronic music and so on, stupidity and imbecility are not only produced by man, but often by machines as well. It is no longer only the human brain that is doing the composing, but a pair of scissors, cutting the tapes to the right length, or the moviola, on which the cancrizans form of a subject is no longer produced by thought, but by moving a lever. It is as if a petty bourgeois were sitting in a spaceship and whose first question when landing on the moon is, "Where is the next post office?"

If you consider, Eisler, how imperfect are our traditional musical notation and musical interpretation, especially by instruments and conductors, then you ought to welcome a method which fixes simultaneously the notation and the interpretation. It is true that the technicalization of composing is still in the laboratory, but shouldn't such efforts be encouraged?

Absolutely, I am for such experiments if they acknowledge their laboratory character. But if they masquerade as art that is a different matter. For example, Stockhausen[4] has produced an electronic, or whatever he calls it, piece of music, taking years to do it. It is based on a part of the Bible "Three men in the burning fiery furnace." Now the language in the Luther translation in this part of the Bible is magnificent, an account of prehistory resistance. What did Stockhausen make of it? The text is purposely made incomprehensible through the manipulation of the tapes, and thus the actual social significance of this part of the Bible is juggled away. What remains to be understood is "Great God on high, we praise Thee."

You must admit, my dear friend, that for something like this I don't need technicalization. The stupidity of this composition, the pompousness of the characters and certain "weird effects" is amazing–hardly to be outdone by Hollywood B-pictures. It shows a retarded social consciousness.

So music is stupid and contradictory if it has no social consciousness?

Theoreticians who refer to the autonomous, abstract development of musical material have forgotten one thing–that music is made by man for man. That does not take place in a vacuum. Music develops in class struggle, for class struggle is the source of all productivity. In music it is more refined and more complex than any ideologist will admit. There is no such thing as the autonomous development of musical material. Music can only develop in the contradictory relationship of music to society. Whoever does not understand that, is a blockhead, no matter how clever he is. The history of music will be written by Marxists. And blockheads will remain blockheads, no matter how clever they may appear to some of us.

Third Series

What causes stupidity in music at the present time?

Aloofness to, disinterest in and aversion to politics.

Are you aware, Eisler, that such an attitude is also a political one?

Of course, and that means decay.

Wasn't that always so?

No. Think of Hegel's description of the myth of Prometheus. "But already the appointed day had come on which
it was necessary for man to come up out of the earth into
daylight. Now being at a loss to find help for men, he
stole from Hephaestus and Athene both their skill and fire
also (for without fire it was impossible for anyone to possess or use this skill) and so he bestows them on men.
Now in this way man acquired the necessary skill to keep
himself alive but he had no *political* wisdom, for this was
still in the hands of Zeus, and Prometheus had no longer
the right of entry to the citadel of Zeus around whom stood
his frightening sentinels."

Does that concern the "unpolitical" artist?

That about the eagle, too, which tears out Prometheus'
liver and devours it, if you think what boozers our musicians are. Hegel goes on: "But he goes stealthily into the
dwelling shared by Hephaestus and Athene in which they
practised their art, and after stealing the art of working
with fire from Hephaestus and the other (the art of weaving) from Athene, he gives these arts to men. And through
this gift men had the means of life but Prometheus, thanks
to Epimetheus, later, as is told, suffered punishment for
theft.

"Plato then goes on in the immediately following passage
to relate that men also lacked for their nurture the art
of war against beasts, an art which is only one part of
politics; therefore they collected together in cities, but
there, for want of political skill, they injured one another
and scattered again so that Zeus was compelled to give
them, with Hermes as his messenger, respect for others and
a sense of justice."

Perhaps, Eisler, it is my fault that I read too little Hegel?

It can be a mistake to read too much Hegel. Listen: "Fire and the skills that make use of it are nothing ethical in themselves, and the art of weaving has nothing of the sort either; in the first instance they appear solely in the service of selfishness and private utility without having any bearing on the community of human existence and the public side of life."

Hegel is astonishing!

He is astonishing, if you read him uncritically.

Doesn't the listener also contribute to stupidity in music?

Without question even in our state where educational privileges have been ended, music culture is in its early stages. It is odd to have to confess that it is easier to explain an equation of modern physics, like Albert Einstein's famous $E = mc^2$ and to popularize it than to do the same for the String Quartet in F minor op. 95 by Beethoven.[5] We can build an atomic power station more easily and land on the moon more quickly than we can apprehend the great classical and modern music and make it the property of the working people. For, unfortunately, listening to music requires training. If that does not occur, then listening lags behind the most progressive social consciousness.

For many people that could be an unsuitable remark.

Yes, we often simplify the situation. For there is after all the double error. If some people disregard this statement as unrefined or vulgar, others will think it too sophisticated. They will claim that the healthy reaction of the people will enable them to find their way to great music, and that great music will decline automatically in late capitalism.

*That would be a sort of spontaneity theory in art apprecia-
tion. Here the blossoming, there the decline, that is fine!*

Naturally. But the blossoming must be worked and fought
for daily. We cannot rely too much on history taking its
course. Beware of being presumptuous!

Stupidity in music today takes on artful and amusing
forms. Recently in a discussion with young people I was
suddenly confronted with the Heisenberg theory, the Principle of Indeterminacy,[6] in which Heisenberg had rein-
troduced God and which they thought, might be of great
significance for modern art, including music.

*But Eisler, you could have answered that you don't need
Heisenberg to find God. Haven't the most important musicians in the capitalist countries found their God? Think of
Stravinsky and Hindemith, Messiaen or Křenek, also
Schönberg and Webern, to mention only a few. Stravinsky
gives us no peace until he has prayed to his God in twelve
tones two or three times a year, and the imbecility of
Hindemith's "Harmony of the World"[7] caused pained
disappointment even among the bourgeoisie.*

Maybe, but this religiousness is old-fashioned compared
with the younger ones who are starting to operate with
Heisenberg.

What is Heisenberg's Principle of Indeterminacy?

One point has been taken from the very complex theory,
which vulgarized, means roughly the following: the perception of an object itself changes the perceptual object,
so that it can no longer be recognized. You can see what a
harassed life people like me lead. In order to combat
stupidity in music I have to cope with physics.

You have not defined the Principle of Indeterminacy from

a mathematical-physical standpoint, but from a philosophical one.

That the young people do, too, who have neither the bent nor the interest in mathematics or physics, but in God. But you forget one thing, no matter what Heisenberg thinks about himself, or what he does in practice, he has nevertheless given us Marxists a weapon for driving deism out of art: deism which today is so sordid. Perception for us has always meant change. We cannot work out either what a socialist society will occupy itself with in the year 3000. Today we only know that their problems will be different from ours. Since we are busy building up our socialist production, we are often unable to decide on questions and matters which will arise after the most urgent problems have been solved.

Could you put it this way: if you see a banker in private could the quality of perception change him?

Certainly. You no longer see his function, but a charming man, not without kindliness; his cleverness becomes homely practical wisdom; his brutality becomes an earnest character, steeled in the struggle of life; his crimes become human weaknesses. In short—the Principle of Indeterminacy is in command.

Eisler, we spoke about physicists and bankers, but too little about music.

I think that physicists and bankers play too great a role in music. Our composers don't know that yet, but they will have to learn it.

Source: *Über die Dummheit in der Musik* in *Sinn und Form,* Berlin 1958, Nos. 3, 4, 5, 6.
EGW III/2 (in preparation).
This article was written as an imaginary dialogue.

1 The waltz *Küssen ist keine Sünd* is from the Viennese operetta *Bruder Straubinger,* written in 1903 by Edmund Eysler (1874–1949).

2 Beethoven composed his Third Symphony in 1803–04; it was first performed in 1805.

3 Sigmund Freud's book, *Das Unbehagen in der Kultur* (Civilization and Its Discontents) was first published in 1930.

4 Karlheinz Stockhausen (born 1928) one of the initiators of electronic music, considered one of the authoritative composers of the Federal Republic of Germany. *Gesang der Jünglinge im Feuerofen* for five loudspeaker groups was composed in 1956.

5 Einstein's equation $E = mc^2$ indicates the equivalence of energy (E) and the mass of a body (m) taking into account the velocity of light in vacuum (c).

6 The physicist Werner Heisenberg (1901–1976) established the Principle of Indeterminacy named after him, according to which complementary physical quantities cannot be measured simultaneously with any accuracy. Heisenberg's philosophy was an inconsistent mixture of subjective-idealism and materialism.

7 Paul Hindemith composed his symphonic *Harmonie der Welt* in 1951. Its thematic material is based on medieval numerical symbols supposed to represent cosmic harmony which music reflects in its microcosm.

America's War of Independence –
Indirect Aggression?
1958

You must hand it to Mr. Dulles, he has a way of shooting
off his mouth that would make a big game hunter envious.
Take, for instance, what he calls indirect aggression. In
my youth I composed a wonderful verse by Brecht: *Denn
wenn der Hungernde stöhnend zurückschlägt den Peiniger...* that would be "indirect aggression"[1] in Dulles'
opinion.

When the people sweep away corrupt sheikhs or bought-
off governments,[2] when they smash colonial chains then
according to Dulles these have ceased to be historical
processes, but indeed are "indirect aggression!" Then historically the American War of Independence against England
was "indirect aggression!" The great French Revolution?
What else but "indirect aggression!" For Marxists the
history of mankind is a history of class struggles. For Dulles, the solicitor of the big banks, the history of mankind
is a history of "indirect aggression." The blame for this,
so he thinks, is not to be laid on the peoples who rebel,
but on the Socialist camp, above all, on the Soviet Union,
that is, on us "wicked Communists."

To continue with Brecht: *Denn wenn der Hungernde
stöhnend zurückschlägt den Peiniger, haben wir ihn bezahlt,
daß er stöhnt und zurückschlägt* (For when the man who is
starving groans and hits back at his oppressor we paid
him so that he groans and hits back).[3]

Source: *Neues Deutschland,* August 8, 1958.

1 Here Eisler is obviously referring to a message from
Nikita S. Khrushchev to President Eisenhower regarding
the Middle East crisis of the time. The message was published in *Neues Deutschland* and read in part: "You maintain that the Middle East problem is not a question of
aggression on the part of the U.S.A., but is rather a question of indirect aggression."

2 On July 14, 1958 a bourgeois-democratic revolution in
Iraq had toppled the monarchy and proclaimed a republic.
The rulers of the neighboring states of Lebanon and Jordan
feared a similar development, due to the growing progressive forces in their countries. Pleas for help were used by
the U.S.A. and Great Britain as an excuse to send troops in.
They also feared restrictions in their spheres of influence
and the end of the military bloc created by the Baghdad
Pact. They attempted to justify these actions by claiming
that there was a danger of indirect aggression.

3 Eisler's quotation, "For when the man who is starving
groans and hits back at his oppressor..." is taken from
a choral number of the didactic play *The Measures Taken*
by Brecht and Eisler.

Schweik
and German Militarism
1961

Hanns Eisler, could you please explain to us what the special features of your music to Schweik *in the Second World War are, compared with other incidental music which you wrote to plays by Brecht, for example,* The Mother *and* The Life of Galileo, *both of which were performed by the Berliner Ensemble at the Festival of Nations in Paris?*

The music to Schweik is not incidental music in the conventional sense. It is much more than that. It is the most significant of all the music to plays by Brecht. It is almost a small opera, in the meaning of the term as Brecht used it, or if you like, a musical comedy. For the music in this work has different functions from conventional incidental music and several methods of musical expression were used.

First, there is the music of the "Higher Regions." There you hear the singing of such notorious men as Hitler, Göring, Himmler and a certain General Bock. Bock was the type of Prussian nobility who advised the Führer on "technical questions" warning him to be cautious and who today believes that the war was lost only through the incompetence of an amateur who called himself Adolf Hitler.

In these pieces I make liberal use of Wagner, because he was the favorite composer of the Nazis.

So what these people are singing is deformed opera. The fascist leaders are exposed as bad Wagnerian singers, as small mediocre provincial artists, which they should have remained, instead of becoming the leaders of a people.

The music of the "Higher Regions"—that is sentimentality and worthlessness, the remnants of a false and repugnant romanticism. An aloof music, merciless, wickedly revealing.

The second music level is that of the songs of the people, Baloun's songs, Mrs. Kopecka's and Schweik's own songs. The music is simple and direct, you can remember and whistle it at once.

The dances and pantomiming come third. The dances are the polka, the waltz and the beseda.

If I am not mistaken the nineteenth century patriotic Czech petty bourgeoisie originated the beseda during the movement for their national rebirth against Austrian rule. It was this beseda the guests at the inn, "The Tankard," danced to induce the Germans to leave.

Yes, at that time it was already a form of national resistance to the occupiers. In fact, the music of Hungary and Bohemia at that time was rebellious.

Don't you also have similar seemingly harmless songs in France which are actually revolutionary? For instance *Le temps des cerises* (The Time of the Cherries).

But to come to the fourth level, to the intermezzi and entr'actes. This music is symphonic in character, and includes songs and Czech folk dances, which I personally have heard (when I attended the Prague Military School and in the Czech army during the war in 1916).

Does that result in a mixture of contradictory styles, or in a unity to which everything is subordinated? And is this music something more than just a succession of entr'actes? In which way does the music, in accordance with Brecht's well-known intentions, play a role in the action?

There are no breaks in style, on the contrary, the various elements form a unity. I will give two examples of where the music plays the role of modifying the action. When all the people at "The Tankard," stirred by Baloun's song, start to dance the beseda, this national dance not only expresses their resistance, but is, at the same time, a camouflage. Under cover of the uproar and noise, Mrs. Kopecka, at the risk of her life, is in the back room listening to Radio Moscow. The second example: after the Gestapo have raided the inn and beaten Mrs. Kopecka, just at the right moment a song is heard, like a ray of light in the despair and obscurity. This song is the leitmotiv of the whole play, the "sung" lesson of living dialectics, it is the Song of the Vltava. In other words it is a song in which the way out, the solution is hinted at (for in fact, historically the battle of Stalingrad was still not the end, and the play ends before Stalingrad). And what does the song say? That after twelve hours of night the day is dawning, nothing more, nothing more than the simple law of nature. It is impossible at this moment to give more hope than that. Only a small consolation, but the necessary minimum. It says: our life is changing as the days and times change— History has confirmed the truth of this song.

Doesn't your music also express the special character of Schweik's "resistance" and thus the resistance movement of the Czech people? Wasn't that more of passive resistance?

Yes, it is the music of the resistance, for the main part written during the war. It is true, Czech resistance was different in character to French resistance. (The French partisan movement was more militant, more direct, more heroic if you like.) Although there were also partisans, predominantly in Slovakia. (Slovakia is mountainous so that it was possible to hide, Bohemia, on the other hand, is an industrial area, where you know every stone and so was unsuitable for any kind of Maquis.) But if you talk about passive resistance, I don't agree. The game that Schweik plays with the Gestapo is something, after all! Just think of Paris under the occupation.

Yet in his work notebook Brecht emphasizes that Schweik, the man in the street, is not an insidious saboteur, but honestly approves of the existing order.

Yes, but just as in the original, the Schweik of the First World War, the Schweik of Jaroslav Hašek. The Schweik of the novel gets a whole country into disorder by stubbornly carrying out all the regulations and orders of his superiors. Just imagine if you were to observe to the letter all the safety regulations in a train! The result would be complete chaos.

That is what we call la grève du zèle–*strike, so to speak, by working to rule.*

If you like. Schweik is the acme of artfulness in an undemocratic regime, in a system of oppression, but it is the artfulness of someone naive, who says and does everything completely without guile. That is why he should have a fixed and constant, but quite disarming smile. Brecht says that the face of the good soldier Schweik should shine like the full moon.

In other words: his reliable political instinct takes the place of his lack of political awareness.

Not quite. Right from the very beginning Schweik is a patriot. There is no doubt about that. He acts as a patriot when he exerts every possible effort to restrain his friend Baloun from serving with the Wehrmacht because of the bigger rations.

Or take Schweik's anti-Communist speeches. They are irresistible because all that Schweik does is to repeat the slogans and arguments of the fascists against Communism, and the Soviet Union, without altering a word. Yet coming from him these same slogans and arguments seem absurd and inhuman, idiotic, at any rate to the ears of rational human beings. That is the art of citation applied by Brecht again and again—this citation that unmasks the enemy. It is the brutal illustration to Thomas Mann's dictum: "Anti-Communism is the fundamental folly of our age." Besides, the great Austrian satirist, Karl Kraus, had already spoken of the unmasking citation.

Schweik's and Baloun's undermining activities should not be underestimated, for instance, when he offers for sale photos of destroyed German towns, as if they were pornography. Of course Schweik is quite a small fish, no shark. He slips through the mesh of the fascist nets as well as he can, but sometimes he gets caught up in them. Schweik is on the level of the general national resistance movement. Obviously, his resistance is not the resistance of a class. He is a small dealer.

Do you believe the attitude represented by Schweik in war can also be expedient in peaceful "Zeiten der Grösse?"

Naturally. The "greater" the times, the more cunning the man in the street must be to survive. Yet without irreparable compromises! Without selling himself! Schweik often errs, but never sells himself. Schweik, that is to say the people, cannot be corrupted. Just think of the "friendly advice" he gives to the deserters. You must be sure to bring the Russians something, a machine gun or something of the sort.

But he refuses to go with them!

Because he is afraid of getting involved with provocateurs and stool pigeons (he already got to know one, Brett-schneider). He simply advises them not to go over to the enemy empty-handed. Out of friendship! After that, he continues his march to Stalingrad.

It was a brilliant idea in book and play to portray some-body who carries on until the bitter end—but who at the same time has not the slightest interest in war. But in the

character of Schweik doesn't Brecht make opportunism
appear more shameful under a fascist regime, than under
the Hapsburg monarchy?

Fascism wasn't as harmless as the monarchy. Under fascism
a Schweik could have found himself on the gallows for a
slight infringement.

To conclude: you think that Schweik, a character from the
brain of an anarchist, I mean Hašek, is still topical?

Yes, there are Schweiks everywhere, millions of them. They
are no heroes, but they can be relied upon. That is the
lesson. Despite obscurity the wisdom of the people cannot
be fooled or misled. But naturally, one must not exaggerate
the historical role of Schweik too pedantically. What
Schweik does is not enough; a more conscious, more direct
and stronger resistance is required. That was there too.
Nobody, least of all Brecht, thought of denying that. But
everyone does not necessarily have to have a thorough
political education, in order not to lose hope under a
dictatorship. That is why the "Higher Regions" are always
confronted with the "Small World." In contrast to official
statements and popularity "by command"–"You are loved
by the people" Himmler tells Hitler–you see the sober
reality of the people in the next scene.

Dictators are never loved.

Source: *Schweyk und der deutsche Militarismus* in *Sinn*
und Form, special issue on Hanns Eisler, Berlin 1964,
pp. 271–75.
EGW III/8 (in preparation).
The talk with the French specialist on German language
and literature, André Gisselbrecht, took place on October

11, 1961 in Berlin in the composer's home, preparatory to the Paris production of Brecht's play, *Schweyk im zweiten Weltkrieg*. It was published in *La Nouvelle Critique*, Sept./Oct. 1961, under the heading, *Entretien avec Hanns Eisler*.

Eisler wrote the music to *Schweyk* in several stages. Some of the songs had already been written during his exile in America *(Und was bekam des Soldaten Weib, Kälbermarsch)*. The first complete version, which was finished in 1956, had its première in Warsaw at the Polish Army Theater (Jan. 17, 1959). It contained the songs of the second level and the dances of the third musical level. The intermezzi were added for the performance in Frankfort on the Main in 1961 and the music of the "Higher Regions" was added in the same year for the performance in France.

Thoughts
on Form and Content
1962

We must be clear about the uses and limitations of theory
for the composer. If a composer is not master of his craft,
then the best theories will not help him. I have been teaching for nearly forty years, yet if I were not able, pencil in
hand, to show a pupil how to do it better, then I would
only be talking generalities and that would not suffice.
When we theorize, we, as Marxists, are clear about the uses
and limitations of theory.

We composers too, should occupy ourselves with Hegel's
theories on aesthetics. They are difficult to read. I would
say, restrict yourself at first to the chapter on music.

Let us take Hegel's distinction between objectivity and
subjectivity in music. Let me give some examples: the high
form of subjective expression in the interpretation of the
text of the Mass in Beethoven's "Missa Solemnis" and in
Bach's Mass in B minor. Beethoven inserts belligerent
music in his "Dona nobis pacem." So it becomes clear that
it is not only a question of individual reconciliation with
God, but of real war and peace on earth. The wonderful
"Dona nobis pacem" in the B minor Mass by Bach is more
of a reconciliation, of an atonement. Beethoven is more
lucid here, one could almost say more realistic than Bach.
But let us be glad that we have two such masterly works.
Nevertheless, while we are glad we should not forget to
assess them differently.

I would like you to acquire a taste for Hegel, and
consequently for Marx too. Just let me quote from memory:

"It is possible that in a society finally freed, art will die away. Philosophy will take its place." That is a prodigious sentence. Is it an impertinence of the philosopher towards us artists? Hegel means that with the progressing consciousness of man—and here we should amplify him by adding a mankind finally freed and at the highest stage of material and cultural development—the production of art might be more inclined to die away than to increase. And when Hegel says philosophy, perhaps he means the new consciousness of a mankind as yet undreamed of who no longer needs the semblance of beauty. That sounds rather abstruse, but it is comprehensible if one thinks about it, and why shouldn't composers think occasionally?

The terms *Volk* and *Volkstümlichkeit* are thoroughly respectable with us, but since I discovered class society through Marx my advice would be to treat these terms in music rather more carefully. I believe much licence is taken here.

In his famous essay on the poet Bürger, Schiller said that although he did not want to annoy Bürger with the term of popularity, all the same the task of classical art was to close the gap between the educated and the people. And Schiller accuses Bürger of writing down to the people. Now we know that this gap cannot be bridged from above. For great social changes have broken the monopoly of education and made possible the bridging of this gap.

If we want to re-establish the terms "people" and "popularity," then we must realize that the people are formed anew only after smashing class rule. The term "popularity" is not inflexible, but developing. The aim of our popularity must be to make the most complicated works of the classics and the moderns generally understood. That I understand as a new kind of popularity, not the old, worn out and conventional one.

The development of music proceeds in a peculiar contradiction—in progress and recession simultaneously. That should be explained.

Philipp Emanuel Bach's piano sonatas seem to us primitive compared with the suites and preludes of Johann Sebastian Bach. They are primitive in formal continuity, in structure, in harmony and modulation. Despite this they contain progressive elements, namely, a new kind of emotional music-making, from the technical point of view, with contrasting ideas and subjects. In order to develop new elements, other elements have to recede. This contradictory procedure is often to be found in the history of music and it must be understood as such. For instance, in the Mannheim Symphonic School we find a new expressiveness. Compared with the great baroque suites it was an extraordinarily simple music, yet something new had been discovered, contrast of themes in one movement with modulations, a new kind of instrumentation. The crescendo and decrescendo in the orchestra was developed, the tremolo in the strings was discovered. Reports say that when the audience heard a string tremolo for the first time they jumped up from their seats, it was such a sensation. Here, the new symphonic style is a changeover from the complicated music of the baroque to simplicity. However, this new simplicity was the basis for the development of the great classical school of Haydn, Mozart and Beethoven. In Beethoven's late works simplicity again changes over towards complexity, the results of which are still felt today.

We have seen in the history of music that a new content can be achieved through a change in the musical device, but this can no longer be discerned in the most recent phase of development. That should make us think twice. Take the following examples: the love-death scene from the last act of *Tristan und Isolde*[1] by Wagner; the final aria in *Salome*[2] by Richard Strauss; and Schönberg's monodrama, *Die Erwartung*. All three have this in common: great arias, disintegrated form, illustration, leitmotiv technique, highly soporific music. In all three of these great arias, despite the change in the use of musical material, there has been no further change in the function of music. The composers keep to "psychologizing" and illustrating. One could go still further and now produce such pieces by means of twelve tone music, serially, electronically. The function would remain the same, a psychologizing, soporific music. This is where our discernment starts and that of the petty-bourgeois composers stops. It can't go on like this.

For us it is above all a question of changing the purpose and function of music. Not by using more and more intoxicating devices, but by using devices in a more reasonable way. What we have to do is clarify the emotions of our listeners, not to confuse them. The worst thing I can think of is music that causes emotional confusion. Even that archaic, intoxicating "musical" element which all music contains must be utilized consciously and not spontaneously.

How poor we musicians have become, if we look back at prehistory of music which we can do through legends and myths of antiquity and the Bible. What power music had. Just think of the trumpets of Jericho, of Orpheus, of Odysseus and the Sirens. As we know, the Sirens were fabled beings (half woman–half bird) who sat on a rock and with their beautiful singing lured the sailors to their doom. (A pale copy of the Sirens is to be found in the well-known song "The Loreley.")[3] In the Homer legends we see, not without emotion, how beauty can lead to destruction. But the cunning Odysseus, the widely traveled merchant, outwits the Sirens. He stops up the ears of his sailors with pitch and has himself bound to the mast. In this way he could enjoy the beauty of the music without succumbing. That would be like a bank director having himself chained to his seat during the last movement of the Ninth

Symphony (All mankind will be brothers) to prevent himself from handing his wallet to his neighbor.

Think of the great Orpheus, whose music turns stones into houses, tames animals and subdues the underworld, but turns women to Furies, who in turn tear him to pieces.

These myths are full of subtleties and are contradictory, not easy to grasp. Every generation interprets them differently. But one thing is clear to us today, the more primitive the society, the stronger was the power of music and of art in general. The more man masters nature, the more progressive his consciousness becomes, the less influence has art on human consciousness. Thus art changes its function. Out of the mythical and ritual, art becomes pleasure and is refunctioned to enrich our lives.

But for socialist composers that is no excuse to avoid or underestimate the tasks facing music today in a socialist society. We shall only succeed if we make use of all the wisdom of both the old and the new. Don't treat it lightly.

Source: *Inhalt und Form* in *Musik und Gesellschaft*, Berlin 1962, No. 9. pp. 541–46.
EGW III/2 (complete transcription of tape recording in preparation).
Eisler gave an extemporaneous talk on March 9, 1962 at the Composers and Musicologists Union of the G.D.R. on the subject of Form and Content. This was Eisler's last public appearance. The article comprises excerpts from the talk which was published by *Musik und Gesellschaft*, edited by Eisler.

1 *Tristan und Isolde* (1857–59), which in his use of musical means, is Richard Wagner's most daring opera.

2 The opera, *Salome* by Richard Strauss was composed in the years 1903–05, Schönberg's monodrama, *Die Erwartung* in 1909.

3 *Die Lorelei*, is one of the best-known German folk songs, music by Friedrich Silcher, words by Heinrich Heine.

Chronology

1898   Born July 6 in Leipzig, son of Austrian philosopher Dr. Rudolph Eisler.

1901   Family removed to Vienna.

1916   Eisler drafted into the Austrian Army.

1919–1923   Studied with Arnold Schönberg.
Eisler conducted workers' choirs in Vienna.

1922   Composed Sonata for Pianoforte for Two Hands, op. 1 (dedicated "To Arnold Schönberg in deepest admiration"). Six Songs for Voice and Pianoforte, op. 2 (dedicated "To Dr. Anton Webern").

1924   Eisler awarded the Art Prize of the City of Vienna.

1925   Removal to Berlin.

1926   First compositions for workers' choirs: Three Male Voice Choruses, op. 10 to words by Heinrich Heine.
Zeitungsausschnitte (Newspaper Cuttings) for voice and pianoforte; with this composition Eisler took his "farewell of bourgeois concert lyricism."

1927   Began his creative work for the revolutionary working-class movement.
Eisler became music critic of *Rote Fahne* (Red Flag), central organ of German Communist Party; joined the leading agit-prop group

Das Rote Sprachrohr (Red Spokesman) as pianist and composer. Wrote his first film music to Walter Ruttmann's experimental film *Opus III.*

Collaboration began with Bertolt Brecht, Erich Weinert, Ernst Busch etc. Compositions for Erwin Piscator's theater.

1928   Eisler wrote his first incidental music to Lion Feuchtwanger's play, *Kalkutta, 4. Mai,* which included his first composition of a text by Brecht – *Ballade vom Soldaten* (The Soldier's Ballad).

1928–1932   Composition of numerous mass songs and worker's choruses, also film and incidental music.

1930   December 13 – First performance of the didactic play, *Die Massnahme* (The Measures Taken), by Brecht with Eisler's music.

1931   Composed music to *Kuhle Wampe oder Wem gehört die Welt* (Whither Germany?), film script by Brecht. The *Solidaritätslied* (Solidarity Song) was part of the film music.

1932   January 17 – First performance of Brecht's *Die Mutter* (The Mother), music by Eisler. In spring *Kleine Sinfonie,* op. 29 (Little Symphony), was written.

              In May Eisler traveled to the Soviet Union to work on the film, *Komsomol (Song of Heroes),* directed by Joris Ivens.

1933   Fascism took power in Germany.
              Eisler forced to emigrate.

1933–1938   Concerts, lectures and other work in Austria, France, Belgium, Holland, England and the U.S.A., Czechoslovakia and the Soviet Union. Frequent visits to Denmark to work with Brecht.

1934	December – Composed *Einheitsfrontlied* (United Front Song) in London at the suggestion of International Revolutionary Theatre Association, Moscow.
1935	February and May – Eisler visited U.S. for the first time. Six proletarian culture organizations arranged lecture and concert tour. Eisler spoke at more than 50 mass meetings on the effects of fascism in Germany, appealing for solidarity with Saar refugees, who had fled Nazi occupation. Eisler's fighting songs were sung at these meetings by soloists and choirs conducted by Eisler and others.
	June 8–10 – First International Workers' Music Olympiad in Strasbourg.
	June 15 – Music Festival at Königshöhe near Reichenberg, Czechoslovakia. Both festivals to promote international united front against fascism and war in which Eisler played important role.
	October 1935 – April 1936 – Eisler held two courses on "Composition," and "The Crisis in Modern Music," at the New School for Social Research in New York. Eisler and Brecht prepared the Theatre Union's production of *The Mother* in New York.
	Gave concerts and made gramophone records.
1936–1947	Work on the *Deutsche Symphonie,* texts by Brecht.
1937	January – Eisler traveled to Spanish front, composed songs for International Brigades and organized concerts.
	In summer, 9 chamber cantatas were written in Denmark, and the "Lenin" Requiem to a text by Brecht.
1938	January 21 – Eisler arrived in U.S.A. for

third time, now with intention of staying. He had again been invited to lecture at the New School for Social Research.

1939	April – Went to Mexico City for teaching assignment at the Conservatoire. September – Returned to New York for film work.
1940	February 1, 1940 – March 30, 1943 – Eisler worked on "A Study of Music in Film Production," a project financed by Rockefeller Foundation. In this connection Eisler composed some of his most masterly works, which were refunctioned for concert works: the chamber music, *Fourteen Ways of Describing Rain,* op. 70; the *Chamber Symphony,* op. 69; and the *Suite für Septett,* No. 1, op. 92a *(Variations on American Children's Songs).* The theories resulting from the Studies appeared in *Composing for the Films,* written together with Theodor W. Adorno, Oxford University Press.
1941	Summer – The collection of pieces for female or children's choir was written in Woodbury, Conn., known as Woodbury Songs.
1942–1943	*Hollywood Songbook,* 50 songs for voice and pianoforte, texts by Brecht, Anacreon, Hölderlin, Goethe, Rimbaud and others.
1944	March 2 – Eisler awarded "Oscar" for the "Best music score of a dramatic or comedy picture" for the film, *Hangmen also Die,* (idea, Brecht/Wexley, director, Fritz Lang).
1946	November – In connection with campaign against the "Communist agent," Gerhart Eisler, a slanderous campaign began in the U.S. press against Hanns Eisler as well.

1947	May 11 and September 24 – Eisler appeared before the House Committee on Un-American Activities. The chief investigator accused Eisler of being the "Karl Marx of Communism in the musical field."
	December 14 – A concert was held as part of solidarity campaign for Eisler. A petition from 14 renowned artists and scientists to Attorney General, Tom Clark, demanded deportation hearing against Eisler be dropped.
1948	February 6 – In a short formal hearing Eisler received his deportation order.
	February 28 – A big farewell concert, organized by the Eisler Committee was held at Town Hall, New York.
	March 26 – Eisler departed. After short stays in London and Prague, Eisler moved to Vienna.
1949	Lecture and concert tours in the Soviet Occupation Zone of Germany. Eisler composed the national anthem of the German Democratic Republic, founded on October 7, 1949.
1950	Eisler moved to the G.D.R. He accepted a professorship at the College of Music in Berlin, which today bears his name, and took over a Master Class for Composition at the Academy of Arts.
	Eisler wrote the *Neue Deutsche Volkslieder* (New German Folksongs), with Johannes R. Becher.
1950–1962	The following were among his many compositions for film and theater:
	Films – *Der Rat der Götter* (1950), *Frauenschicksale* (1952), *Herr Puntila und sein Knecht Matti* (Vienna 1955), *Nuit et brouil-*

lard (Paris 1956), *Die Hexen von Salem* (Paris 1957).

Theater – Shakespeare: *Hamlet* (1954), Becher: *Winterschlacht* (1955), Brecht: *Die Gesichte der Simone Machard* (1955), Brecht: *Die Tage der Kommune* (1956), Majakovski: *Das Schwitzbad* (1958), Brecht: *Schweyk im 2. Weltkrieg* (1959), Schiller: *Wilhelm Tell* (1962).

1957   The cantata, *Die Teppichweber von Kujan-Bulak* (The Carpet-weavers of Kuyan-Bulak), composed to Brecht's text.

1959–1961   Composed 36 poems by Kurt Tucholsky, at the suggestion of Ernst Busch.

1962   Eisler finished the *Ernste Gesänge* (Serious Songs) for baritone and string orchestra, after texts of classical and contemporary poets shortly before his death on September 6, 1962.

Eisler was twice awarded the National Prize, in 1950 and 1958.

In addition to single editions of his instrumental works, the ten volume edition of his *Lieder und Kantaten* was started (Breitkopf und Härtel Musikverlag, Leipzig, 1955). Since 1968, the Hanns Eisler Archives of the Academy of Arts of the G.D.R. have been issuing a collected edition of his writings entitled, *Hanns Eisler, Gesammelte Werke* (Deutscher Verlag für Musik, Leipzig). Records of his complete works are being produced simultaneously by Deutsche Schallplatten.